Make an
E-commerce Site in a
Weekend

Using PHP

Bintu Harwani

Apress®

Make an E-commerce Site in a Weekend: Using PHP

ISBN-13 (pbk): 978-1-4842-1673-6

ISBN-13 (electronic): 978-1-4842-1672-9

Managing Director: Welmoed Spahr
Lead Editor: Ben Renow-Clarke
Technical Reviewer: Massimo Nardone
Editorial Board: Steve Anglin, Pramila Balen, Louise Corrigan, Jim DeWolf,
    Jonathan Gennick, Robert Hutchinson, Celestin Suresh John, Michelle Lowman,
    James Markham, Susan McDermott, Matthew Moodie, Jeffrey Pepper, Douglas Pundick,
    Ben Renow-Clarke, Gwenan Spearing
Coordinating Editor: Melissa Maldonado
Copy Editor: Kezia Endsley
Compositor: SPi Global
Indexer: SPi Global
Artist: SPi Global

Distributed to the book trade worldwide by Springer Science+Business Media New York, 233 Spring Street, 6th Floor, New York, NY 10013. Phone 1-800-SPRINGER, fax (201) 348-4505, e-mail orders-ny@springer-sbm.com, or visit www.springer.com. Apress Media, LLC is a California LLC and the sole member (owner) is Springer Science + Business Media Finance Inc (SSBM Finance Inc). SSBM Finance Inc is a **Delaware** corporation.

For information on translations, please e-mail rights@apress.com, or visit www.apress.com.

Apress and friends of ED books may be purchased in bulk for academic, corporate, or promotional use. eBook versions and licenses are also available for most titles. For more information, reference our Special Bulk Sales–eBook Licensing web page at www.apress.com/bulk-sales.

Any source code or other supplementary material referenced by the author in this text is available to readers at www.apress.com. For detailed information about how to locate your book's source code, go to www.apress.com/source-code/.

This book is dedicated to:

My mother, Mrs. Nita Harwani. My mother is next to God for me. Whatever I am today is because of the moral values taught by her.

And

Vladimir Kosma Zworykin, Philo Taylor Farnsworth, and John Logie Baird—the inventors of the modern television, commonly referred to as the TV. TV, as we all know, is the most relaxing and entertaining device of today. After a long, tiring day at work, I enjoy sitting in front of the TV and watching my favorite shows.

Contents at a Glance

Contents

About the Author

 **Bintu Harwani** is the founder and owner of Microchip Computer Education (MCE), based in Ajmer, India. It provides computer education in all programming, web developing, and smart phone platforms. He is also a well renowned speaker and author of several books. His latest books include *Foundation Joomla*, published by friends of ED, *jQuery Recipes*, published by Apress, *Core Data iOS Essentials*, published by Packt, *Introduction to Python Programming and Developing GUI Applications with PyQT*, published by Cengage Learning, *Android Programming Unleashed* published by Sams Publishing, *The Android Tablet Developer's Cookbook* (Developer's Library), published by Addison-Wesley Professional, *UNIX & Shell Programming*, published by Oxford University Press, *PhoneGap Build: Developing Cross Platform Mobile Applications in the Cloud*, published by Auerbach Publications, and *Learning Object-Oriented Programming in C# 5.0*, published by Cengage Learning PTR. To learn more, visit his blog at http://bmharwani.com/blog.

About the Technical Reviewer

Massimo Nardone is an experienced Android, Java, PHP, Python, and C++ programmer and technical reviewer. He holds a Master of Science in Computing Science from the University of Salerno, Italy. He worked as a PCI QSA and Senior Lead IT Security/Cloud/SCADA architect for many years and currently works as security, cloud, and SCADA lead IT architect for Hewlett-Packard, Finland. He has more than 20 years of experience in IT, including in security, SCADA, cloud computing, IT infrastructure, mobile, security, and WWW technology areas for both national and international projects. Massimo worked as a project manager, Cloud/SCADA lead IT architect, software engineer, research engineer, chief security architect, and software specialist. He was a visiting lecturer and supervisor for exercises at the Networking Laboratory of the Helsinki University of Technology (Aalto University). He has been programming and teaching how to program with Perl, PHP, Java, VB, Python, and C/C++ for almost 20 years. He holds four international patents (in PKI, SIP, SAML, and Proxy areas).

Acknowledgments

I owe a debt of gratitude to Ben Renow-Clarke, senior web development editor, for his initial acceptance and giving me an opportunity to create this work. I am highly grateful to the whole team at Apress for their constant cooperation and contributions to create this book.

My gratitude to Matthew Moodie, who as a development editor, offered a significant amount of feedback that helped improve the chapters. He played a vital role in improving the structure and quality of the information.

I must thank Massimo Nardone, the technical reviewer, for his excellent, detailed review of the work and the many helpful comments and suggestions he made.

Special thanks to Kezia Endsley, the copy editor, for first class structural and language editing. I appreciate her efforts in enhancing the content of the book and giving it a polished look.

I also thank SPi Global, the formatter, for doing excellent formatting and making the book dramatically better.

Big and ongoing thanks to Melissa Maldonado, the coordinating editor, for doing a great job in getting the book published on time

A great big thank you to the editorial and production staff and the entire team at Apress who worked tirelessly to produce this book. Really, I enjoyed working with each of you.

I am also thankful to my family. Thanks to Anushka (my wife) and my two little darlings—Chirag and Naman—for always encouraging and inspiring me.

I should not forget to thank my dear students who have been good teachers as they make me understand the basic problems they face and help me directly hit those topics. It is because of the endless interesting queries from my students that I was able to write this book with a firmly practical approach.

Introduction

In this book, you will to learn to develop an e-commerce site. Electronic commerce, also known as *e-commerce*, involves purchasing and selling products or services through computers and smart phones using the Internet. Today, almost all businesses need an e-commerce site to sell their products or services and to show their global presence. Hence, most companies show their presence on the Internet by developing e-commerce sites. The e-commerce site that you will be learning to develop in this book will be able to sell almost anything, including books, smart phones, laptops, etc. The site will display different product categories via a drop-down menu along with a search box at the top. Users can select the products and can pay online. The site will store all the products, orders, and customer information in a database.

The book addresses newbie developers who don't have a lot of experience developing web sites. The book teaches you how to display and sell your products and services online. It explains different database tables that will be required for keeping site and customer information. The book explains and takes you through the different stages of developing an e-commerce site. For example, you'll learn to develop different web pages for displaying products, implement a search facility to enable customers to search for products quickly, develop drop-down menus to link different pages of the site, apply authentication checks to customers who are signing in, and associate with payment gateways to accept payments from your customers. The book will be very beneficial for developers and instructors too, who want to learn or teach web site development.

Key Topic Coverage

- Establishing a connection between PHP and MySQL server
- Using HTTP methods for transferring data among web pages
- Applying validation checks on the input forms
- Accessing products and listings and searching desired products
- Creating drop-down menus for the site
- Adding web site headers
- Session handling
- Saving product selections into a cart
- Maintaining the cart
- Supplying shipping information and making payments

A brief description of the content in different chapters of the book is as listed here:

Chapter 1, "Introduction"—In this chapter, you will learn about the benefits of doing e-commerce, that is, selling products and services on the net. You will learn how the final web pages of your e-commerce web site will appear when it's complete. You will also learn to install the WampServer that is required for creating and testing the site. You will see the procedure needed to configure MySQL server via the phpMyAdmin software tool. Also, you will get an idea of the structure of different database tables that will be required so that your e-commerce site will work efficiently.

Chapter 2, "PHP and MySQL"—This chapter explains how the PHP and MySQL combination is used for developing an e-commerce site. You will learn the steps for writing and running your first PHP script. Also, you will learn to pass information from one PHP script to another. You will learn to display forms to get information from the user. Also, you will learn about the methods that are required in establishing connections between PHP and MySQL server. You will learn to write scripts for storing user information into database tables. You will also learn about the methods required for accessing information from the tables and eventually you'll use that knowledge to authenticate a user, by writing a sign-in script.

Chapter 3, "Accessing the Database Using PHP"—This chapter explains the technique of accessing products from a products table and displaying them on-screen in tabular format. You will also learn to create a drop-down menu that displays different product categories and implements navigation from one page to another. You will learn to display products of specific categories, define a web site header, implement a search facility, and display detailed information of the selected product. You will also learn how session handling is done in a web site. You will learn to define the home page of your site, which will show the different product images with the fading effect.

Chapter 4, "Managing the Shopping Cart"—In this chapter, you will learn how the chosen products are saved into the cart table after keeping track of the visitor's session ID. You will also learn to manage the cart content on the visitor's requirement. You will also learn to display the cart count (product quantities selected in the cart) and the visitor's sign-in status on the site's header. You will learn to supply the shipping information, accept payments, and save the chosen products into orders and orders_details database tables.

CHAPTER 1

■ ■ ■

Introduction

In this book, you will learn how to develop an e-commerce site. Electronic commerce, also known as e-commerce, involves purchasing and selling products or services through computers/smart phones using the Internet. Today, almost all businesses need an e-commerce site. Why? Here are a few reasons:

- Selling online does not require office space or any product display space.

- You can sell 24/7/365; no store time constraints.

- Consumers can purchase when it's convenient from their home and at any time. They can save a lot of time wasted in travelling to the store in traffic.

- You can sell your products globally.

- Quick, convenient, and user-friendly transfer of funds online.

Hence, most companies are showing their presence on the Internet by developing e-commerce sites. The e-commerce site that you will be learning to develop in this book will sell almost everything, including books, smart phones, laptops, and so on. The site will display different product categories via a drop-down menu along with a search box at the top. Users can select the products and can pay online. The site will store all the products, orders, and customer information in the database.

Although you can create a web site quite easily through the free e-commerce web design tools provided by different web site hosting providers, doing so has the following limitations:

- The design tool may not be that flexible. The menu, table, and other interfaces might not suit your requirements.

- You might face issues like database connectivity and other authentication processes.

- You might not get support to fetch information for web site administrative tasks.

- It will be very difficult for you to change your web host if you get the site built through its patented tools.

Hence, you will be developing this e-commerce site from scratch in PHP. In this chapter, you will learn:

- The outline of the e-commerce web site that will be made throughout the book

- The software required for developing the site

- Installing the WampServer

- Configuring MySQL

- Details of the database tables that will be required in web site

Why PHP?

PHP stands for "PHP Hypertext Preprocessor" and is one of the most popular web scripting engines among developers. The question is, why is it so popular?

The reasons are many, but the first one is that it is a server-side scripting language, so all PHP scripts are executed on the server instead of the client's machine. Consequently, the script execution does not consume the client's resources but the server's. You will see some client-side JavaScript code in this book also, where it's appropriate and makes sense to use it.

The PHP script runs on the server and its output is sent to the client as plain HTML, which makes it very secure. The visitor of your web site can never see the PHP source code by selecting the View Source option in the browser. The visitor can only view the output from the PHP script, which is plain HTML.

Besides this, PHP supports many databases (MySQL, Informix, Oracle, Sybase, Solid, PostgreSQL, Generic ODBC, etc.). So you can store the customer's information, visitor's information, and your service and product information into the database and then retrieve them whenever required.

PHP is open source software (OSS) and so is freely available. You don't have to pay for using PHP. Moreover, a mass community is involved in developing and enhancing PHP features. This ensures faster bug fixing and availability of enhanced features.

PHP commonly runs on an open source platform, called LAMP. The full form of LAMP is Linux, Apache, MySQL, and PHP. Again, being open source, you get the continuous support of developers around the world for the platform.

PHP can be easily embedded with HTML tags and scripts. So, the code that's not very important can be written in HTML and the crucial code can be written in PHP. The combination runs faster than code that is written purely in PHP.

PHP runs on any platform—Linux, Unix, Mac OS X, and Windows. Besides this, PHP has a garbage collector and an efficient memory manager that optimizes the memory consumption of any site.

How the E-Commerce Site Will Appear

Let's have a quick look at the final result of this book. The e-commerce site that you will be developing throughout this book will appear as shown in the following figures.

The first screen on execution of the shopping cart site that you'll see is shown in Figure 1-1.

Figure 1-1. The first screen upon launching the e-commerce site

You can see that at the top is a header that contains the title of the web site and a Cart icon at the top-right corner (a handy tool for users to know what they have selected in their carts). Below the header is a drop-down menu that displays the list of product categories that are available on the site (see Figure 1-2).

Figure 1-2. *Drop-down menu showing different product categories*

If you select a category, say Laptops, to see all the products in the category, you get the output shown in Figure 1-3.

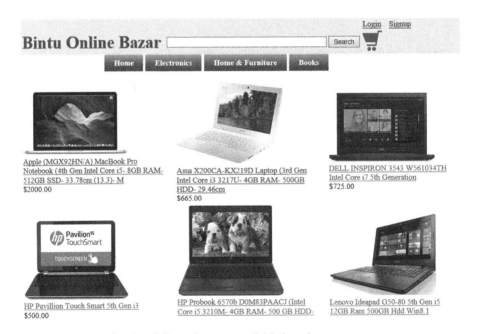

Figure 1-3. *Page showing different laptops available for sale*

The product image and its name include a link that, when clicked, will display detailed information on the selected product. For example, on clicking the Asus X200CA-KX219D laptop, its detailed information will be displayed, as shown in Figure 1-4.

Figure 1-4. *Page showing detailed information of the selected laptop*

The Quantity text box is where you enter how many of the selected product you want. If you leave it blank and click the Add To Cart button, the default quantity is 1. Suppose you want to purchase one selected laptop, you can either enter the value 1 in the Quantity text box, followed by clicking the Add To Cart button, or you can also directly click the Add To Cart button because the default quantity is always 1.

The selected item, along with the entered quantity, is added to the cart as shown in Figure 1-5.

Figure 1-5. *Items selected in the cart*

You can always change the quantity of the product selected in the cart. Also, you can delete any item from the cart. To change the quantity of the Asus laptop in the cart to 2, modify its value in the Quantity column and click the Change Quantity button. The quantity and the total price will change in the cart, as shown in Figure 1-6.

Figure 1-6. *Quantity of the item in cart has changed*

You can even purchase more items belonging to another category. Suppose you need to see all the items under the Smartphone category, you select the category from the drop-down menu on the top. All the products in the Smartphone category will be displayed, as shown in Figure 1-7.

Figure 1-7. *Page showing different smart phones available for sale*

Again, each product's image and name includes a link which, when clicked, displays detailed information about the selected product.

If you click on the Micromax-Canvas-Knight-2-E471 smart phone, its detailed information will appear as shown in Figure 1-8.

Figure 1-8. *Page showing detailed information about the selected smart phone*

Again, the Quantity text box specifies how many of the item you want to purchase (the default value is 1). Assuming you want one of the selected products, click the Add To Cart button. On clicking the Add To Cart button, all the products selected in the cart will be displayed, as shown in Figure 1-9.

Item Code	Quantity	Item Name	Price	Total Price		
AsusX200CA-KX219D	2	Asus X200CA-KX219D Laptop (3rd Gen Intel Core i3 3217U- 4GB RAM- 500GB HDD- 29.46cm	665.00	1,330.00	Change quantity	Delete Item
MicromaxKnight2E471	1	Micromax-Canvas-Knight-2-E471-White	210.00	210.00	Change quantity	Delete Item
Total	3			1,540.00		

You currently have 3 product(s) selected in your cart

Empty Cart   Checkout

Figure 1-9. *Items selected in the cart*

As mentioned, not only can you update the quantity of any product that is selected in the cart, but you also can delete any item from the cart if it is not required. Assume you don't want the Micromax smart phone anymore, for example. To delete it from the cart, click the Delete Item button in that product's row. The Micromax smart phone will be removed from the cart, leaving the two Asus laptops in the cart (see Figure 1-10).

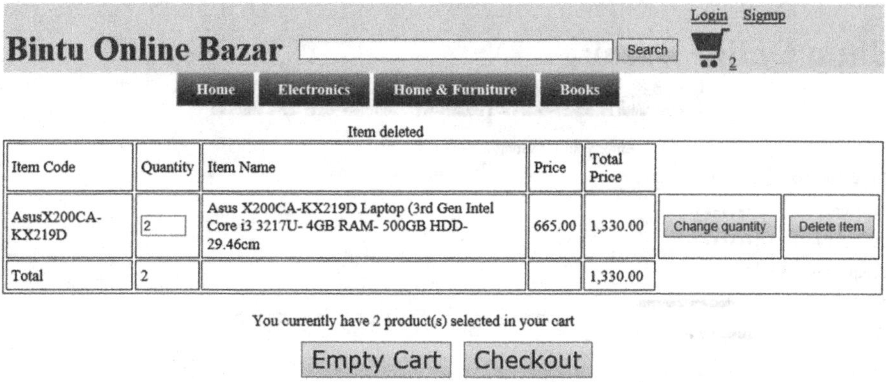

Figure 1-10. An item deleted from the cart

■ **Note**   Clicking the Empty Cart button will remove all the products currently in the cart.

If you are ready to purchase your items, you can click the Checkout button. If before you began shopping, you created an account and logged in, your user details like your name, address, contact number, and so on, will be automatically displayed. The app will just ask for shipping information. But If you are not logged in yet, you will get the message shown in the Figure 1-11.

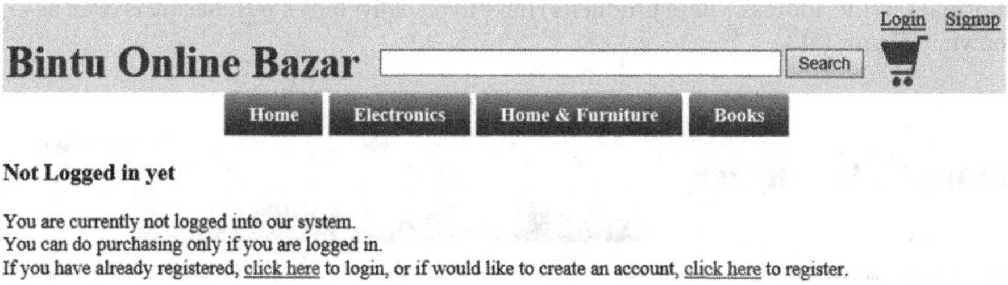

Figure 1-11. Page informing the login status of the customer

If you have not yet created an account, you're prompted to do that first. If you have an account, you will be prompted to log in. If you select the create account link ("click here to login"), you get a screen to fill in user details, as shown in Figure 1-12.

Bintu Online Bazar

Login   Signup

Search

Home   Electronics   Home & Furniture   Books

Enter your information

Email Address:	bmharwani@yahoo.com
Password:	••••••••
ReType Password:	••••••••
Complete Name	Bintu Harwani
Address:	
City:	Ajmer
State:	Rajasthan
Country:	India
Zip Code:	305001
Phone No:	×

Submit   Cancel

Figure 1-12. *Page for creating account of the customer*

While you're filling in the form, be careful to fill in the two fields, Password and ReType Password. These fields must be exactly the same. If the content of these fields don't match, you will be asked to enter them again.

After entering the required information, you are required to click the Submit button. If the supplied information is correct, you'll be registered and asked to provide shipping information (the address where product(s) have to be delivered) if purchasing is over, as shown in Figure 1-13.

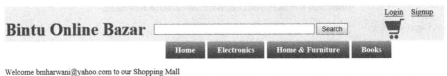

Bintu Online Bazar

Login   Signup

Search

Home   Electronics   Home & Furniture   Books

Welcome bmharwani@yahoo.com to our Shopping Mall
If you have finished Shopping Click Here to supply Shipping InformationOr You can do more purchasing by selecting items from the menu

Figure 1-13. *Welcome message for the signed-in customer*

When you select the link for supplying shipping information, you get a few text boxes to indicate where your products should be delivered, as shown in Figure 1-14.

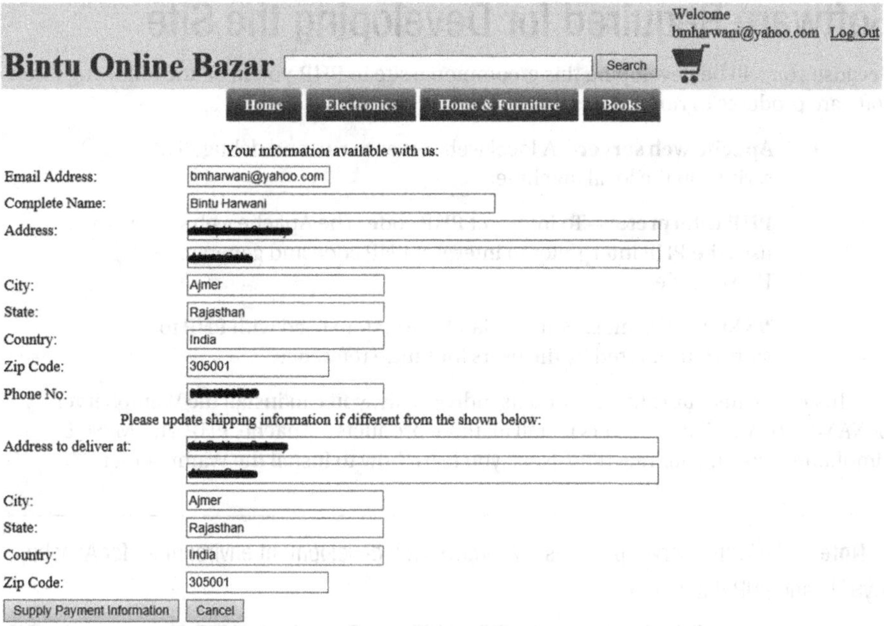

Figure 1-14. *Page for supplying shipping information*

After filling in the shipping information, you click the Supply Payment Information button. You will be taken to a page that asks you to enter payment information, as shown in Figure 1-15.

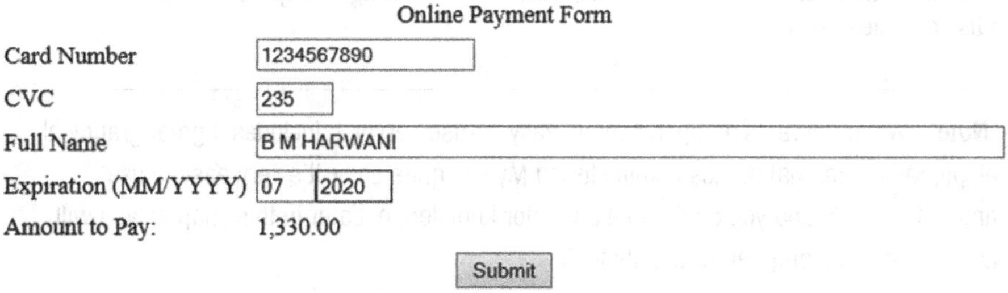

Figure 1-15. *Page for entering payment information*

On clicking the Submit button, the order details will be stored in the database along with a unique order number. This order number is displayed to the users for future communication.

Software Required for Developing the Site

Because you will be developing this e-commerce site in PHP, you need the following three software products to run a PHP script:

- **Apache web server**—A local web server to run and debug PHP scripts on the local machine.

- **PHP interpreter**—To interpret PHP code. The Apache web server uses the PHP interpreter to interpret PHP code and generate HTML code.

- **MySQL**—The most popular database system used with PHP to store data entered by the users for future reference.

Instead of installing these products individually, you can install the WampServer or XAMPP server. These servers install all three products—Apache, PHP, and MySQL—simultaneously on your machine. Next, you learn how to install the WampServer.

■ **Note** The WampServer provides a Windows web development environment for Apache, MySQL, and PHP databases.

Installing the WampServer

To check and debug your PHP scripts locally before uploading to the actual server, you need to install the WampServer on the local machine. So, download a free copy of WampServer from http://www.wampserver.com/en. The latest version of WampServer available at the time of this writing is 2.5. After downloading WampServer, double-click on its .exe file and select Run.

■ **Note** WampServer is an open source, easy-to-use server. It includes a great graphical tool, phpMyAdmin, that makes administering MySQL quite easy. It's very easy to use WampServer tools and you don't need any prior knowledge. Later in this chapter, you will learn how to use WampServer and its tools.

The first screen is a welcome screen that indicates which WampServer version will be installed, as shown in Figure 1-16. Click on the Next button.

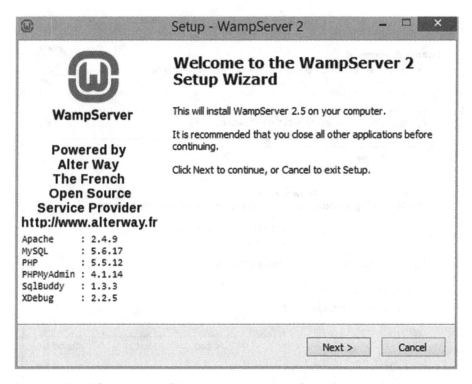

Figure 1-16. *Welcome screen of WampServer setup wizard*

The next window shows the license and terms and conditions of using the WampServer (see Figure 1-17). Accept the license agreement and click Next.

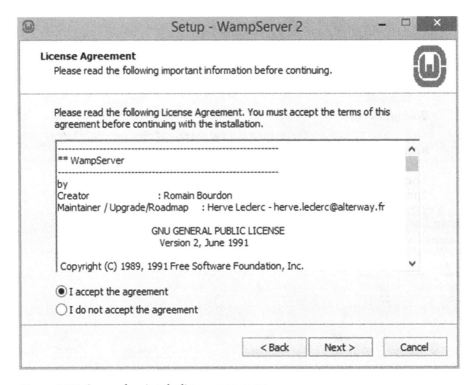

Figure 1-17. *Screen showing the license agreement*

Select the folder to install WampServer (see Figure 1-18). It's best to keep the default folder location. Click the Next button.

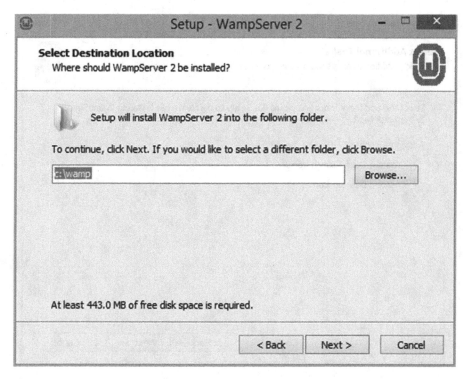

Figure 1-18. *Screen prompting for the installation folder*

Check boxes will be displayed (see Figure 1-19) prompting whether you want to have WampServer icons added to your desktop and to Quick Launch. Check the check boxes. Click Next to move further.

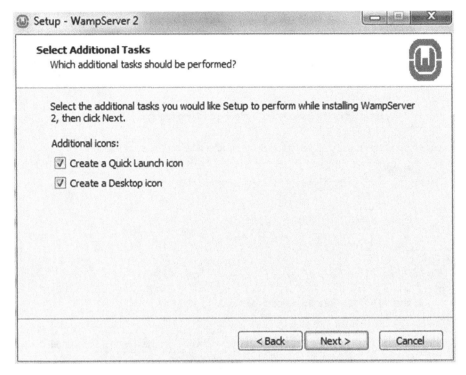

Figure 1-19. Screen prompting whether to show quick launch and desktop icons

The next window shows the items for review that you have chosen up until now. You can click the Back button to make any changes. Let's click the Install button to initiate the installation procedure (see Figure 1-20).

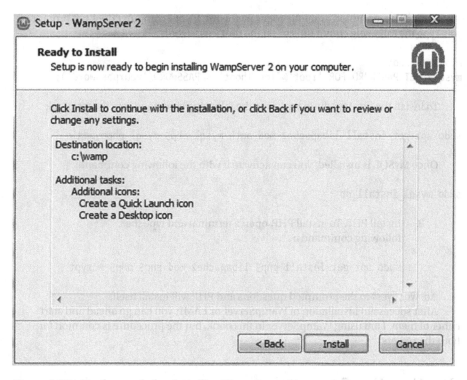

Figure 1-20. Final screen before installing WampServer files

If you have Linux installed on your machine, you can download and install the LAMP server.

Installing the LAMP Server

LAMP stands for Linux, Apache, MySQL, and PHP. It is a group of open source software products used to run a web server on a Linux machine. The following are the steps to install LAMP:

1. Install Apache. To install Apache, open a terminal and type the following commands:

```
sudo apt-get install apache2
```

To check if Apache is installed, open the browser and point at the address http:// localhost/. If the page displays the text, "It works!", Apache was installed successfully.

2. Install MySQL. To install MySQL, open a terminal and type the following commands:

```
sudo apt-get install mysql-server
```

17

You will be prompted to set the root's password. If your computer does not prompt you, type the following commands to set the root's password:

```
mysql -u root
mysql> SET PASSWORD FOR 'root'@'localhost' = PASSWORD('yourpassword');
```

To install the phpMyAdmin tool, type the following command into the terminal:

```
sudo apt-get install libapache2-mod-auth-mysql php5-mysql phpmyadmin
```

Once MySQL is installed, you can activate it with the following command:

```
sudo mysql_install_db
```

3. Install PHP. To install PHP, open a terminal and type the following commands:

   ```
   sudo apt-get install php5 libapache2-mod-php5 php5-mcrypt
   ```

Answer, "yes" to the prompted questions and PHP will install itself.

After successful installation of WampServer or LAMP, you can go ahead and start either of them. I am using WampServer in this book, but the procedure is common for both the servers.

Starting the Server

To use the WampServer, you need to start it. So, either double-click its icon from the desktop or follow these steps:

1. Open the Start screen.

2. From the list of tiles displayed on the Start screen, locate WampServer. If you don't find the WampServer in the list of apps and programs, type the text, WAMP, on the blank space of the screen.

3. A search box will appear and will list all the apps matching the typed text.

4. Click on the WampServer icon shown in the resulting list.

After starting the WampServer, an icon appears in the task bar, as shown in Figure 1-21.

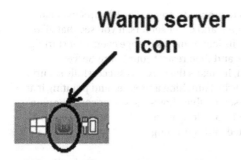

Figure 1-21. WampServer icon displayed in task bar

When the WampServer icon is red, it means no services on it are currently running. When it is orange, it means the WampServer is started, but not all of its services are running. When it's green, that means the WampServer is started and all its services are running correctly. To start the server, click on its icon and select the Start All Services option from the menu that pops up (see Figure 1-22).

Figure 1-22. WampServer popup menu

As the server starts up, it will go from red to orange to green. The WampServer can conflict with the default Skype settings, IIS server, and other servers. If you see that all of the WampServer services are not running, i.e. its icon remains orange even after starting it, you need to stop your IIS server, quit Skype, and then restart your WampServer.

If the WampServer icon changes to green, it means the server is successfully set up and is fully functioning. You can also verify this by launching a browser and pointing it at the `http://localhost` address. If you get the screen that shows the server configuration, Apache version, PHP version, etc. (see Figure 1-23), along with the loaded extensions, it means the WampServer is successfully installed and is running.

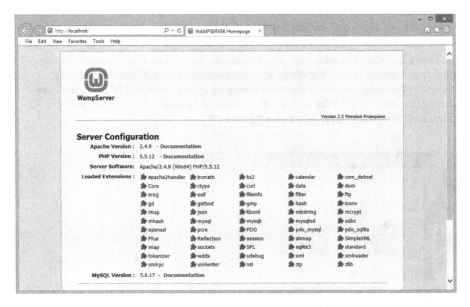

Figure 1-23. *Browser showing server configuration on successful installation of WampServer*

Congratulations, your WampServer is installed successfully. It also means that Apache, MySQL, and PHP are successfully installed on your machine.

By default, WampServer does not set a password for MySQL's root user. To implement security and to avoid unauthorized access, you need to set a password for MySQL's root user and create other users if required. So, let's proceed to configure the MySQL server.

Configuring MySQL

You will be using phpMyAdmin for configuring the MySQL server. phpMyAdmin is a software tool written in PHP, used to administer MySQL over the web. You can easily manage MySQL databases, tables, indexes, users, etc. through phpMyAdmin's graphical user interface. To invoke phpMyAdmin, click the WampServer icon and select the phpMyAdmin option.

phpMyAdmin will open up, as shown in Figure 1-24. The screen shows recent databases in the left pane. At the top right, you will find buttons to manage databases, SQL, users, etc. The middle pane shows the drop-down list that enables you to define the MySQL connection. You will also find the drop-down lists to change the default language, theme, font size, and other settings.

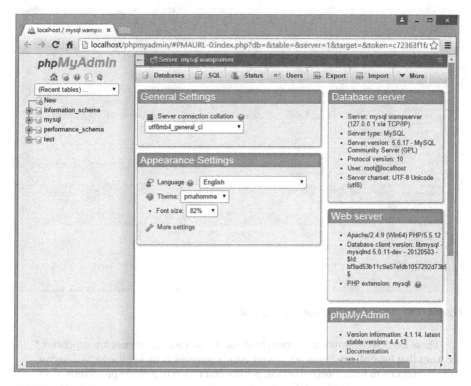

Figure 1-24. *First screen on launching the phpMyAdmin tool*

To configure root's password, you need to access the user table that is found in the mysql database found in the left pane. The + (plus symbol) on the mysql database node indicates that currently it is in collapsed mode. To expand the node, click on its + symbol. The mysql database node will expand showing all the tables that exist inside it. Click the user table to display the number of rows within it (see Figure 1-25). You can see that the user table contains the following four users by default:

- User root for Host, 127.0.0.1—Represents the root user for localhost without resolved IP for IPv4.

- User root for Host, ::1—Represents the root user for localhost without resolved IP for IPv6.

- User root for Host, localhost—Represents the root user for localhost with resolved IP.

- User anonymous for host, localhost—Represents the anonymous user with resolved IP.

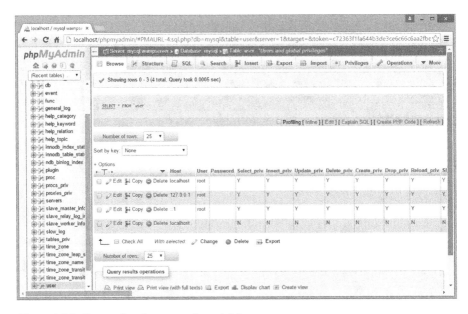

Figure 1-25. Screen showing rows of user table

These users have empty passwords by default. The root usernames are superuser accounts that have all privileges but having empty passwords makes the MySQL server quite vulnerable to unauthorized access. So, the first task is to provide passwords to all these root accounts and either delete the anonymous user or provide a password for that user account too.

To provide passwords to the root users, click on the Edit icon on the respective row to edit its content. The row will open and show the three text boxes—Host, User, and Password. Enter the password in the Password column (see Figure 1-26). If you want to encrypt the password (instead of saving it in the plain text format), select the PASSWORD option from the Function combo box. After entering the password, click the Go button at the bottom to save the changes.

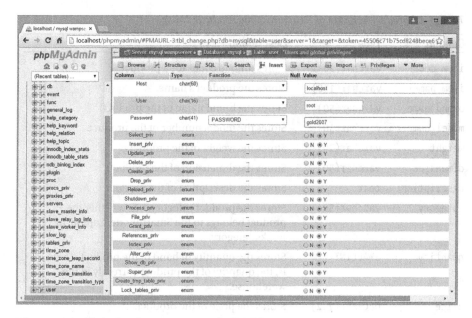

Figure 1-26. *Changing the root password of MySQL server*

Once the password is set for all the root users, your MySQL server becomes quite secure from unauthorized access. Let's learn about the different database tables that will be required in your e-commerce site next.

Required Database Tables

In all there will be seven tables created for our e-commerce site with the following names:

- products—Stores information about the product that includes product name, weight, price, description, etc.

- productfeatures—Stores features of the products.

- cart—Stores information of the products selected in the cart.

- customers—Stores information about the registered customers.

- orders—Stores order numbers, order data, and shipping information of the customer who placed the order.

- orders_details—Stores the information about all the products that are purchased in a given order.

- payment_details—Stores the card number and other information about the payment mode selected to pay for any order.

You will be creating these tables in a database called shopping. The structure of these mentioned tables is explained in Tables 1-1 to 1-7.

Table 1-1. *Brief Description of Structure of the Products Table*

Column	Type	Description
item_code	varchar(20)	Stores unique codes for a product.
item_name	varchar(150)	Stores the product's name.
brand_name	varchar(50)	Stores the brand name of the product.
model_number	varchar(30)	Stores the model number of the product.
weight	varchar(20)	Stores the weight of the product.
dimension	varchar(50)	Stores the dimension of the product.
description	text	Stores the description of the product.
category	varchar(50)	Stores the product category, i.e., whether the product belongs to the Smartphone, Laptop, or Books category.
quantity	SMALLINT	Stores the quantity in hand of the product. That is, the quantity of the product currently in the warehouse.
price	DECIMAL(7,2)	Stores the price of the product.
imagename	varchar(50)	Stores the path and name of the product image.

Table 1-2. *Brief Description of the Structure of the productfeatures Table*

Column	Type	Description
item_code	varchar(20)	Stores a unique code for each product.
feature1/ feature2/ feature3/ feature4/ feature5/ feature6	varchar(255)	Stores the features of the product

Table 1-3. *Brief Description of the Structure of the Cart Table*

Column	Type	Description
cart_sess	char(50)	Stores the session ID of the customer.
cart_itemcode	varchar(20)	Stores a unique code of the product selected by the customer in the cart.
cart_quantity	SMALLINT	Stores a quantity of the product selected in the cart.
cart_item_name	varchar(100)	Stores the name of the product that is selected in the cart.
cart_price	DECIMAL(7,2)	Stores the price of the product that is selected in the cart.

Table 1-4. *Brief Description of theb Structure of the Customers Table*

Column	Type	Description
email_address	varchar(50)	Stores the e-mail address of the registered customer. The e-mail address is considered to be unique for each customer
password	varchar(50)	Stores the password of the registered customer.
complete_name	varchar(50)	Stores the complete name of the registered customer.
address_line1	varchar(255)	Assuming the customer's address is big, this field stores the first address line of the registered customer.
address_line2	varchar(255)	Stores the second address line of the registered customer.
city	varchar(50)	Stores the city name to which the customer belongs.
state	varchar(50)	Stores the state to which the customer belongs.
zipcode	varchar(10)	Stores the ZIP code of the city to which the customer belongs.
country	varchar(50)	Stores the country name of the customer.
cellphone_no	varchar(15)	Stores the cell phone number of the registered customer.

Table 1-5. *Brief Description of the Structure of the Orders Table*

Column	Type	Description
order_no	int(6)	Keeps the order number of the order placed by the customer. The order number is auto generated and is 1 plus the previous order number.
order_date	date	Stores the date on which the customer placed the order.
email_address	varchar(50)	Stores the e-mail address of the customer placing the order.
customer_name	varchar(50)	Stores the complete name of the customer placing the order.
shipping_address_line1	varchar(255)	Stores the first shipping address line where products have to be delivered.

(continued)

Table 1-5. *(continued)*

Column	Type	Description
shipping_address_line2	varchar(255)	Stores the second shipping address line where products have to be delivered.
shipping_city	varchar(50)	Stores the city name where products have to be delivered.
shipping_state	varchar(50)	Stores the shipping state.
shipping_country	varchar(50)	Stores the shipping country.
shipping_zipcode	varchar(10)	Stores the ZIP code of the region where products have to be delivered.

Table 1-6. *Brief Description of the structure of orders_details Table*

Column	Type	Description
order_no	int(6)	Keeps the order number of the order placed by the customer.
item_code	varchar(20)	Stores the product code that is selected in the order.
item_name	varchar(100)	Stores the product name that is selected in the order.
quantity	SMALLINT	Stores the quantity of the product that is selected in the order.
price	DECIMAL(7,2)	Stores the price of the product that is selected in the order.

Table 1-7. *Brief Description of the Structure of the payment_details Table*

Column	Type	Description
order_no	int(6)	Keeps the order number for whom payment is being made.
order_date	date	Keeps the date on which the given order was placed.
amount_paid	DECIMAL(7,2)	Stores the amount that is paid for the given order.
email_address	varchar(50)	Stores the e-mail address of the customer doing the payment.
customer_name	varchar(50)	Stores the name of the customer who is doing the payment.

(continued)

Table 1-7 (continued)

Column	Type	Description
payment_type	varchar(20)	Stores the mode of payment, i.e. whether the customer is paying through debit card, credit card, net banking, etc.
name_on_card	varchar(30)	Stores the name on the debit/credit card if the customer is paying with a card.
card_number	varchar(20)	Stores the credit card number.
expiration_date	varchar(10)	Stores the expiry date of the card (if customer is paying with a card).

Don't worry; you don't have to create these database tables and the shopping database manually. I have provided a SQL script called creatingtables.sql with this book. The SQL script is shown in Listing 1-1.

Listing 1-1. SQL Script, creatingtables.sql

```
create database shopping;
use shopping;
create table products (
    item_code varchar(20) not null,
    item_name varchar(150) not null,
    brand_name varchar(50) not null,
    model_number varchar(30) not null,
    weight varchar(20),
    dimension varchar(50),
    description text,
    category varchar(50),
    quantity SMALLINT not null,
    price DECIMAL(7,2),
    imagename varchar(50)
);

create table productfeatures (
    item_code varchar(20) not null,
    feature1 varchar(255),
    feature2 varchar(255),
    feature3 varchar(255),
    feature4 varchar(255),
    feature5 varchar(255),
    feature6 varchar(255)
);
```

```
create table cart (
    cart_sess char(50) not null,
    cart_itemcode varchar(20) not null,
    cart_quantity SMALLINT not null,
    cart_item_name varchar(100),
    cart_price DECIMAL(7,2)
);

create table customers (
    email_address varchar(50) not null,
    password varchar(50) not null,
    complete_name varchar(50),
    address_line1 varchar(255),
    address_line2 varchar(255),
    city varchar(50),
    state varchar(50),
    zipcode varchar(10),
    country varchar(50),
    cellphone_no varchar(15),
    primary key(email_address)
);

create table orders (
    order_no int(6) not null auto_increment,
    order_date date,
    email_address varchar(50),
    customer_name varchar(50),
    shipping_address_line1 varchar(255),
    shipping_address_line2 varchar(255),
    shipping_city varchar(50),
    shipping_state varchar(50),
    shipping_country varchar(50),
    shipping_zipcode varchar(10),
    primary key (order_no)
);

create table orders_details (
    order_no int(6) not null,
    item_code varchar(20) not null,
    item_name varchar(100) not null,
    quantity SMALLINT not null,
    price DECIMAL(7,2)
);

create table payment_details (
    order_no int(6) not null,
    order_date date,
    amount_paid DECIMAL(7,2),
```

```
    email_address varchar(50),
    customer_name varchar(50),
    payment_type varchar(20),
    name_on_card varchar(30),
    card_number varchar(20),
    expiration_date varchar(10)
);
```

You need to just run this script to create the database and tables. Follow the next steps to do so.

Steps to Run the MySQL Script

To run the SQL script, you need to open the MySQL console. So, click the WampServer icon in the task bar and select the MySQL->MySQL console option from the menu that pops up.

You will be asked to enter the user root's password. After entering the password, you will be greeted with the mysql> prompt in the MySQL console window, as shown in Figure 1-27.

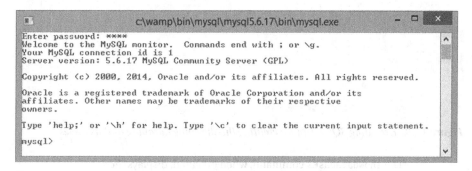

Figure 1-27. MySQL console window for running SQL commands/scripts

To execute a SQL script, you need to use the source command. The syntax for the source command is:

```
source [path] sqlscript.sql
```

Assuming the creatingtables.sql file is placed in the D: drive, you can execute it using the following command:

```
source D:\\creatingtables.sql
```

The SQL commands in the creatingtables.sql file will execute and will create the shopping database and the tables discussed previously. For each successful execution of SQL command, you get the Query OK output, as shown in Figure 1-28.

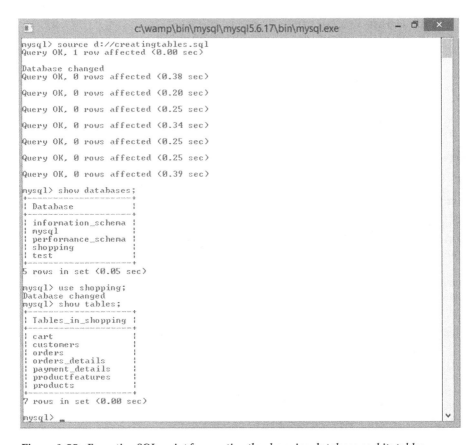

Figure 1-28. Executing SQL script for creating the shopping database and its tables

- The showdatabases command, when executed, displays the existing databases in the MySQL server. The shopping database confirms that the shopping database is successfully created.

- The use command makes the specified database the active or current database. The use shopping SQL command makes the shopping database active.

- The show tables command, when executed, displays all the tables that exist in the currently active database. You can see that all the seven database tables are successfully created in the shopping database.

After the successful creation of database and its tables, you need to fill in some dummy product information in the products and productsfeatures tables. To do so, you need to execute another SQL script provided with this book, called insertingrows.sql. This is done in exactly the same was as for the creatingtables.sql script.

Summary

In this chapter, you learned how the final e-commerce web site will appear when it's complete. Also, you saw how to install WampServer, which is required for creating and testing this site. You also learned how to configure MySQL server via the phpMyAdmin software tool. Finally, you saw the database structure of the different tables that are required for saving information about the products, orders, and customers for this web site.

In the next chapter, you will learn how to write your first PHP script. Also, you will learn to pass information from one PHP script to another. Using this knowledge, you will learn to create a sign-in form for creating new user accounts.

CHAPTER 2

■ ■ ■

PHP and MySQL

You are going to use PHP and MySQL for developing this e-commerce site. The question is why PHP and MySQL? The answer is very simple. The PHP and MySQL combination makes the web development task quite easy. A few of their features are listed here:

- Both are open source technologies and are available under the GPL (General Public License). Consequently the cost of developing web applications in this combination is quite low.

- PHP is a powerful language and connects with MySQL server quite easily, making the combination popular for web development.

- The combination can be successfully used under UNIX as well as Windows platforms.

- Performance of the combination is quite high. The code written in PHP for inserting and fetching information from MySQL is very efficient.

- PHP and MySQL are widely supported by the developer community, so you get regular updates.

In this chapter, you will learn about the following:

- Writing your first PHP script

- Using variables in PHP, creating an echo statement, and concatenating strings

- Using HTTP methods to transfer data—GET and POST

- Passing information from one script to another using $_GET, $_POST and $_REQUEST arrays

- Creating a sign-in form

- Applying validation checks

- Writing code for connecting PHP with MySQL

- Executing SQL commands through PHP, storing information in the database table, and accessing information from the database

- Implementing authentication

33

Writing Your First PHP Script

A PHP file normally contains HTML tags and some PHP scripting code embedded in it. The simplest PHP script that displays PHP's configuration is shown in Listing 2-1. Before you learn the procedure to run this script, you should have a quick idea about the phpinfo() function that is used in this script.

The phpinfo() function displays information about PHP's configuration. It displays information that includes the following:

- PHP compilation options

- PHP version

- Server information and environment

- PHP environment

- Different values of configuration options

- PHP license

Listing 2-1. PHP Script (phpdetails.php) to Display the PHP Configuration Information

```php
<?php
        phpinfo();
?>
```

To run this PHP script, follow these steps:

1. Type this script using any editor and save it using the phpdetails.php name in the www subfolder of the wamp directory. For example, if WampServer is installed on the C: drive, save this script in the C:\wamp\www folder.

2. Make sure that WampServer is running, i.e., its icon in the task bar is green. If it's not, click on its icon and select Start All Services from the menu that pops up.

Once WampServer starts running, open the browser and point at the following address: http://localhost/phpdetails.php. You will get the output as shown in Figure 2-1.

PHP Version 5.5.12

System	Windows NT BINTU1 6.2 build 9200 (Windows 8 Business Edition) AMD64
Build Date	Apr 30 2014 11:15:47
Compiler	MSVC11 (Visual C++ 2012)
Architecture	x64
Configure Command	cscript /nologo configure.js "--enable-snapshot-build" "--disable-isapi" "--enable-debug-pack" "--without-mssql" "--without-pdo-mssql" "--without-pi3web" "--with-pdo-oci=C:\php-sdk\oracle\x64\instantclient10\sdk,shared" "--with-oci8=C:\php-sdk\oracle\x64\instantclient10\sdk,shared" "--with-oci8-11g=C:\php-sdk\oracle\x64\instantclient11\sdk,shared" "--enable-object-out-dir=../obj/" "--enable-com-dotnet=shared" "--with-mcrypt=static" "--disable-static-analyze" "--with-pgo"
Server API	Apache 2.0 Handler
Virtual Directory Support	enabled
Configuration File (php.ini) Path	C:\WINDOWS
Loaded Configuration File	C:\wamp\bin\apache\apache2.4.9\bin\php.ini
Scan this dir for additional .ini files	(none)
Additional .ini files parsed	(none)
PHP API	20121113
PHP Extension	20121212
Zend Extension	220121212
Zend Extension Build	API220121212,TS,VC11
PHP Extension Build	API20121212,TS,VC11
Debug Build	no
Thread Safety	enabled
Zend Signal Handling	disabled
Zend Memory Manager	enabled
Zend Multibyte Support	provided by mbstring
IPv6 Support	enabled
DTrace Support	disabled
Registered PHP Streams	php, file, glob, data, http, ftp, zip, compress.zlib, compress.bzip2, https, ftps, phar
Registered Stream Socket Transports	tcp, udp, ssl, sslv3, sslv2, tls
Registered Stream Filters	convert.iconv.*, mcrypt.*, mdecrypt.*, string.rot13, string.toupper, string.tolower, string.strip_tags, convert.*, consumed, dechunk, zlib.*, bzip2.*

This program makes use of the Zend Scripting Language Engine:
Zend Engine v2.5.0, Copyright (c) 1998-2014 Zend Technologies
  with Xdebug v2.2.5, Copyright (c) 2002-2014, by Derick Rethans

Powered By

Figure 2-1. *PHP script displaying PHP configuration information*

Next, a very basic example that displays two lines of text in the output is shown in Listing 2-2.

Listing 2-2. Simple PHP Script (phpscript1.php)

```
<html>
    <head>
    </head>
    <body>
        <h1>Bintu Online Bazar</h1>
        <?php
            echo '<b>Welcome to our store</b>';
        ?>
    </body>
</html>
```

Again, save this script as `phpscript1.php` in the `www` subfolder of the `wamp` directory. Make sure that WampServer is running, and then open the browser and point at the following address: `http://localhost/phpscript1.php`. You will get the output shown in Figure 2-2.

Figure 2-2. *PHP script displaying the welcome message*

In the code shown in Listing 2-1, you can see that a PHP script can be easily embedded with HTML using the opening PHP tag, `<?php` and the closing PHP tag, `?>`.

On finding a PHP script, the web server invokes the PHP engine and passes the script to it. The PHP engine interprets the statements enclosed between the `<?php` and `?>` tags, generates the corresponding HTML code, and passes it back to the web server. The web server sends the HTML document to the client's browser for display.

A PHP scripting block can be placed anywhere in the document and each statement must end with a semicolon. The semicolon is a separator and is used to distinguish one statement from another.

For storing values and text, you need variables. So, next we'll discuss variables.

Using Variables in PHP

Variables may be used to store the data entered by the user or to store constant numerical values or text. The variable's value is assigned with the help of the assignment operator (=). All variables in PHP start with a dollar ($) sign symbol. The script shown in Listing 2-3, phpscript2.php, demonstrates how variables are defined and used in PHP.

Listing 2-3. PHP Script Demonstrating Using Variables (phpscript2.php)

```
<html>
    <body>
        <?php
            $name="John";
            echo "Welcome $name <br/>";
            $a=10;
            $b=20;
            echo "Sum of $a and $b is ";
            echo $a+$b;
        ?>
    </body>
</html>
```

Output

```
Welcome John
Sum of 10 and 20 is 30
```

The most commonly used statement in PHP scripts is echo. It's covered next.

The echo Statement

The echo statement is used for displaying the output on the client's browser at the current location in the HTML code. The output can be displayed with single quotes, double quotes, or no quotes:

- **Single quotes**—To display message without any variable or arrays. Example:

  ```
  echo 'Welcome to our store';
  ```

- **No quotes**—To display value/text assigned to a variable, you don't need to use quotes. For example, the following lines display text assigned to the variable msg.

  ```
  $msg = 'Welcome to our store';
  echo $msg;
  ```

- **Double quotes**—To display value/text assigned to a variable within a string. Example:

```
$msg = 'Welcome to our store';
echo "Hello! $msg";
```

Concatenating Strings

To concatenate two or more string variables together, use the dot (.) operator. The script in Listing 2-4, phpscript3.php, shows how two strings are concatenated.

Listing 2-4. PHP Script Demonstrating String Concatenation (phpscript3.php)

```
<html>
    <body>
        <?php
            $a="John";
            echo "Hello $a!" . " Welcome to our store";
        ?>
    </body>
</html>
```

Output:

```
Hello John! Welcome to our store
```

In this script, you can see that the first string, "Hello John!", is concatenated to another string, "Welcome to our store" by making use of the dot operator (.) in between.

■ **Note**   In PHP, you use // to make a single-line comment. For comments extending more than a line, enclose them between a pair of /* and */ symbols.

HTTP Methods for Transferring Data

While developing applications, you might come across a situation where you want the data entered by the users on one web form to be supplied to another for further processing or action. The information from one web form to another is usually passed by two HTTP request methods called GET and POST.

The GET Method

This is the default method of passing data and is considered to be less secure, as it is displayed in the browser's address bar. When you see something like this in the browser's address bar:

`display.php?name=john&email_add=john@yahoo.com`

It means the data is being passed using the GET method to the `display.php` script. The data that is being passed has two variables—name and `email_add`. Data passed through the GET method is visible to everyone and is also stored in the browser's history/logs, making it less secure. So, the GET method is typically used to pass unimportant data.

The GET method supports only ASCII characters, hence you cannot pass binary information using this method. Moreover, there is a limit on the amount of information passed through this method. It can be a maximum of 2KB. Some servers handle up to 64KB.

When the HTTP GET method is used, data of the previous form is stored in an array called $_GET array. The data is passed in the form of pairs, variable name(s), and values.

The POST Method

In this method, the information passed is more secure as it is not displayed in the browser's address bar. Here are a few of the POST method's features:

- Data is passed directly over the socket connection using secure HTTP protocol, hence data is secure.

- POST method variables are not displayed in the URL. Also, the POST requests do not remain in the browser history.

- No restriction on sending data size.

- Even binary data or ASCII information can be sent.

- When the POST method is used, the data of the current form is collected in the $_POST array.

Passing Information from One Script to Another

To understand the concept of passing of data through the GET and POST methods, you'll make a form that asks the user to enter their name and e-mail address, as shown in Figure 2-3.

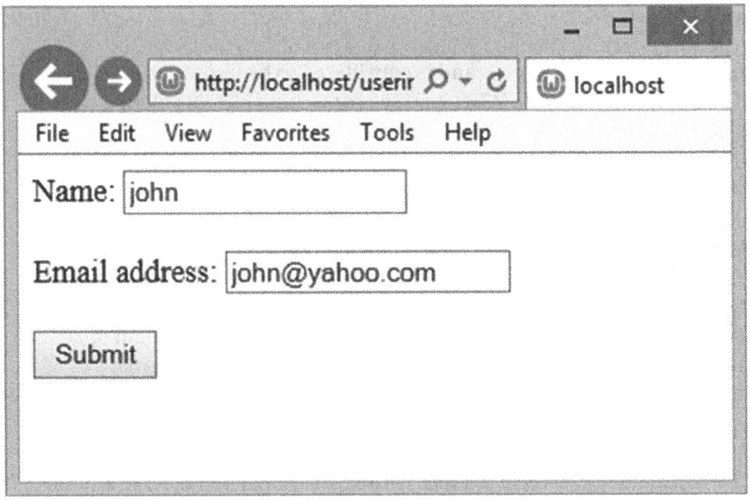

Figure 2-3. Form prompting for name and e-mail address

To create such a form, create a PHP script called userinfo.php with the code shown in Listing 2-5.

Listing 2-5. Form for Entering the Name and E-Mail Address (userinfo.php)

```
<html>
    <head>
    </head>
    <body>
        <form action="display.php" method="Get">
            Name: <input type="text" name="name" /><br/><br/>
            Email address: <input type="text" name="email_add" /><br/><br/>
            <input type="submit" value="Submit" />
        </form>
    </body>
</html>
```

This form has two input boxes named name and email_add. The form action points to a PHP file, display.php. The HTTP method used for passing data (name and email_add) is GET.

To pass information between the scripts, three arrays that act as a carrier of data are $_GET, $_POST, and $_REQUEST. You'll learn how these arrays are used to transmit data one by one.

Using $_GET Array

The $_GET array is where data from the previous form sent using the HTTP GET method is stored. The data from the previous form is sent in the form of pairs: variable name(s) and value(s).

Refer to the form shown in Listing 2-2. When the user clicks the Submit button in it, the URL in the browser's address bar will appear as shown:

```
http://localhost/display.php?name=john&email_add=john@yahoo.com
```

You can see that the URL displays all the information that is being passed. The destination PHP script, display.php, can now extract the data from the $_GET array through the code, as shown in Listing 2-6.

Listing 2-6. Form for Accessing Information from the $_GET Array (display.php)

```
<html>
    <head>
    </head>
    <body>
        Welcome <?php echo $_GET["name"]; ?>.<br>
        Your email address is <?php echo $_GET["email_add"]; ?>
    </body>
</html>
```

This code accesses the name and e-mail address passed by userinfo.php through the $_GET array and displays them on the screen, as shown in Figure 2-4.

Figure 2-4. *Name and e-mail address of the user displayed on another form*

Using $_POST Array

The $_POST array collects the values sent from a form using the HTTP POST method. To pass data using the POST method, you only need to replace GET in the form's method attribute with POST in the userinfo.php script shown in Listing 2-2.

As discussed, in the POST method, the $_POST array collects the values from the form. It also means that when the users click the Submit button, the $_POST["name"] and $_POST["email_add"] variables will be automatically filled with the data they entered in the two boxes.

To display the name and e-mail address in the destination PHP script, display.php, you need to replace the $_GET array with the $_POST array, as shown in Listing 2-7.

Listing 2-7. Form for Accessing Information from the $_POST Array (display.php)

```
<html>
    <head>
    </head>
    <body>
        Welcome <?php echo $_POST["name"]; ?>.<br>
        Your email address is <?php echo $_POST["email_add"]; ?>
    </body>
</html>
```

Besides $_GET and $_POST, there is one more array that is used for storing information about the current form; it's called $_REQUEST.

Using the $_REQUEST Array

The $_REQUEST array contains the content of $_GET and $_POST. That is, it is used to collect the information from a form that's sending data by the GET or POST method.

So, in case you don't know which HTTP method was used by the source PHP script, it is wise to access the information using the $_REQUEST array. To display the name and e-mail address via the $_REQUEST array in the display.php script, you replace $_POST (in Listing 2-7) with $_REQUEST, as shown in Listing 2-8.

Listing 2-8. Form for Accessing Information from the $_REQUEST Array (display.php)

```
<html>
    <head>
    </head>
    <body>
        Welcome <?php echo $_REQUEST["name"]; ?>.<br />
        Your email address is <?php echo $_REQUEST["email_add"]; ?>
    </body>
</html>
```

Now you know how forms are created and through which HTTP methods. Information from one form can also be transferred to another. Next, you'll use the knowledge you've gained so far to create a sign-up form that enables users to register on your site.

Creating the Sign-Up Form

A sign-up form enables users to register on your site. A sign-up form usually prompts users to enter an e-mail address, password, complete name, address, cell phone number, etc. This information is then stored in a database for future use.

Once their data is stored in a database, users don't have to re-enter it. It will be automatically fetched upon a successful login. The PHP script, `signup.php`, is shown in Listing 2-9.

Listing 2-9. Sign-Up Form for Creating a New Account (signup.php)

```
<html>
<head>
</head>
<body>
    <form action="addcustomer.php" method="post">
        <table border="0" cellspacing="1" cellpadding="3">
            <tr><td colspan="2" align="center">Enter your information</td>
            </tr>
            <tr><td>Email Address: </td><td><input size="20" type="text"
            name="emailaddress"></td></tr>
            <tr><td>Password: </td><td><input size="20" type="password"
            name="password"></td></tr>
            <tr><td>ReType Password:  </td><td><input size="20"
            type="password" name="repassword"></td></tr>
            <tr><td>Complete Name  </td><td><input size="50" type="text"
            name="complete_name"></td></tr>
            <tr><td>Address:  </td><td><input size="80" type="text"
            name="address1"></td></tr>
            <tr><td></td><td><input size="80" type="text" name="address2">
            </td></tr>
            <tr><td>City:  </td><td><input size="30" type="text"
            name="city"></td></tr>
            <tr><td>State:  </td><td><input size="30" type="text"
            name="state"></td></tr>
            <tr><td>Country:  </td><td><input size="30" type="text"
            name="country"></td></tr>
            <tr><td>Zip Code:  </td><td><input size="20" type="text"
            name="zipcode"></td></tr>
            <tr><td>Phone No:  </td><td><input size="30" type="text"
            name="phone_no"></td></tr>
```

```
            <tr><td><input type="submit" name="submit" value="Submit"></td><td>
            <input type="reset" value="Cancel"></td></tr>
      </table>
   </form>
</body>
</html>
```

The output of this PHP script is shown in Figure 2-5. You can see that several text boxes are displayed so the users can enter their e-mail addresses, passwords, complete names, address, city, state, country, Zip code, and phone number. The data entered in the respective text boxes is passed to the addcustomer.php script for storing the information in the table. The form is submitted by using the HTTP POST request method. Recall that $_POST is an array that stores the variable names and values sent by the HTTP POST method. It also means that in the addcustomer.php script, the information about the new user will be retrieved via $_POST array.

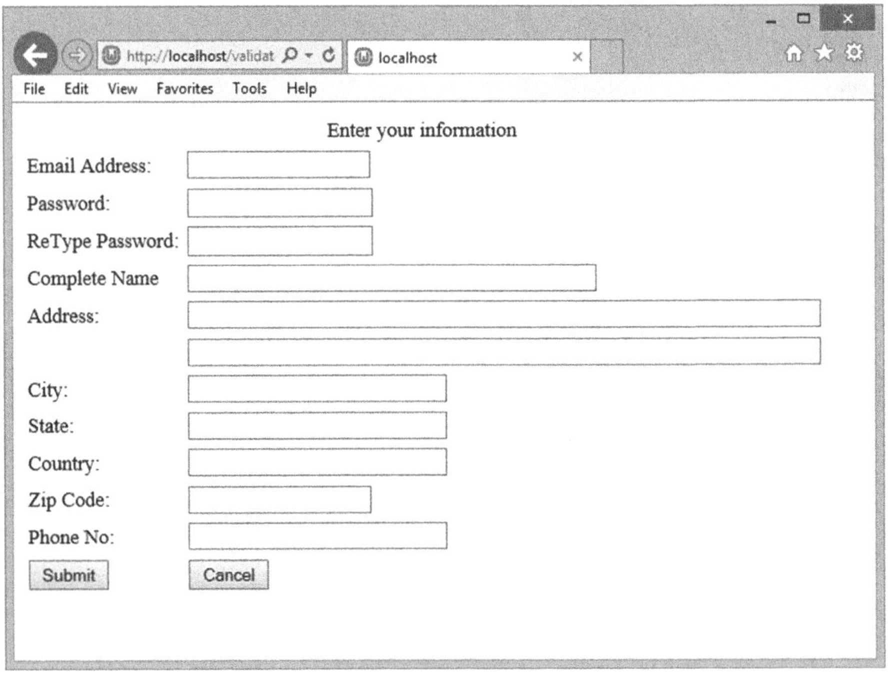

Figure 2-5. *Sign-up form for creating new account*

This PHP script seems perfectly okay if the user supplies essential information like an e-mail address, password, etc. correctly. What if the user leaves some of the essential boxes blank?

The previous PHP script does not apply validation checks. Next, let's learn how to apply validation checks to the sign-up form.

Applying Validation Checks

For providing correct input to your application, data validation is a must. Data validation is the process of ensuring that data entered into a web form is correct and in the desired format. Data validation includes checking whether:

- Data is entered in the required fields. No essential field is left blank.

- No mistake is made when entering data. For example, no text is entered into a numerical field and vice versa.

- Data is entered in the desired format. For example, a date is entered in the required format.

You will be using JavaScript to apply validation checks to the sign-up form. The PHP script, validatesignup.php, is shown in Listing 2-10.

Listing 2-10. Sign-Up Form for Creating a New Account (validatesignup.php)

```
<html>
<head>
<script language="JavaScript" type="text/JavaScript" src="checkform.js">
</script>
</head>
<body>
    <form action="addcustomer.php" method="post" onsubmit="return
    validate(this);">
        <table border="0" cellspacing="1" cellpadding="3">
            <tr><td colspan="2" align="center">Enter your information</td></tr>
            <tr><td>Email Address: </td><td><input size="20" type="text"
            name="emailaddress" ><span id="emailmsg"></span></td></tr>
            <tr><td>Password: </td><td><input size="20" type="password"
            name="password" ><span id="passwdmsg"></span></td></tr>
            <tr><td>ReType Password:  </td><td><input size="20"
            type="password" name="repassword"><span id="repasswdmsg">
            </span></td></tr>
            <tr><td>Complete Name  </td><td><input size="50" type="text"
            name="complete_name" ><span id="usrmsg"></span></td></tr>
            <tr><td>Address:  </td><td><input size="80" type="text"
            name="address1"></td></tr>
            <tr><td></td><td><input size="80" type="text" name="address2">
            </td></tr>
            <tr><td>City:  </td><td><input size="30" type="text"
            name="city"></td></tr>
```

```
            <tr><td>State:   </td><td><input size="30" type="text"
            name="state"></td></tr>
            <tr><td>Country:   </td><td><input size="30" type="text"
            name="country"></td></tr>
            <tr><td>Zip Code:   </td><td><input size="20" type="text"
            name="zipcode"></td></tr>
            <tr><td>Phone No:   </td><td><input size="30" type="text"
            name="phone_no"></td></tr>
            <tr><td><input type="submit" name="submit" value="Submit">
            </td><td>
            <input type="reset" value="Cancel"></td></tr>
        </table>
    </form>
</body>
</html>
```

The first statement to mention imports the JavaScript file, checkform.js, into the current web page:

```
<script language="JavaScript" type="text/JavaScript" src="checkform.js">
</script>
```

JAVASCRIPT

Because JavaScript is used in this chapter, you need a quick introduction to it.

JavaScript is a programming language that is used for extending a web site's functionality by allowing for dynamic pages and implementing validation checks. A few of JavaScript's features are:

- It's a lightweight, interpreted programming language.

- It usually executes on the client machine, hence it consumes less server resources and avoids excessive server traffic.

- It's quite fast in delivering responses. Because it processes and executes on the client's machine, it delivers the response faster than other server-side scripting languages.

- It is relatively easy to learn because its syntax is close to English.

The JavaScript file, checkform.js, contains the code to validate different fields in the validatesignup.php file.

There are two ways to include JavaScript in a web page:

- Place the JavaScript in the <head> element.

- Place the JavaScript in a separate file, save it with the extension
  .js, and then use the <script> element to include the code file.
  (By including the JavaScript file, its code will be merged in the
  HTML at that location.) This approach is preferred, as it keeps
  HTML code clean and all the JavaScript code in one place

onsubmit="return validate(this);" invokes the validate() function found in
the JavaScript file and carries this (the current form as an argument) so that all of its
fields can be validated in the validate function. Also, the form will be submitted and will
navigate to the addcustomer.php script only if the validate function returns true. If the
function returns false (if any of the fields fail in validation), form submission will not
take place. Instead, an error will be displayed and the user will be prompted to validate
the field.

<span id="emailmsg"></span> defines a location with an ID and an emailmsg
that will be used to display error messages if the user enters the wrong e-mail address
in the e-mail address box. Similarly, the locations are defined with IDs passwdmsg,
repasswdmsg, and usrmsg for the consecutive boxes to display error messages if the
password, re-type password, and complete name boxes do not validate.

The JavaScript file, checkform.js, applies validation checks on the sign-up form,
validatesignup.php. It's shown in Listing 2-11.

Listing 2-11. JavaScript File (checkform.js)

```
function validate(userForm) {
    div=document.getElementById("emailmsg");  // #1
    div.style.color="red";                     // #2
    if(div.hasChildNodes())                     // #3
    {
        div.removeChild(div.firstChild);        // #4
    }
    regex=/(^\w+\@\w+\.\w+)/;                   // #5
    match=regex.exec(userForm.emailaddress.value);
    if(!match)
    {
        div.appendChild(document.createTextNode("Invalid Email"));  // #6
        userForm.emailaddress.focus();          // #7
        return false;                            // #8
    }
    div=document.getElementById("passwdmsg");
    div.style.color="red";
    if(div.hasChildNodes())
    {
        div.removeChild(div.firstChild);
    }
```

```
if(userForm.password.value.length <=5)  // #9
{
    div.appendChild(document.createTextNode("The password should
    be of at least size 6"));
    userForm.password.focus();
    return false;
}
div=document.getElementById("repasswdmsg");
div.style.color="red";
if(div.hasChildNodes())
{
    div.removeChild(div.firstChild);
}
if(userForm.password.value != userForm.repassword.value) // #10
{
    div.appendChild(document.createTextNode("The two passwords
    don't match"));
    userForm.password.focus();
    return false;
}
var div=document.getElementById("usrmsg");
div.style.color="red";
if(div.hasChildNodes())
{
    div.removeChild(div.firstChild);
}
if(userForm.complete_name.value.length ==0) // #11
{
    div.appendChild(document.createTextNode("Name cannot be blank"));
    userForm.complete_name.focus();
    return false;
}
return true;
}
```

When the Submit button is clicked, the validate() method is invoked. It checks whether the data is entered correctly in the respective text boxes. The document. getElementById() method is used for searching a web form for an object with the specified ID. The object placed anywhere on the form with the given ID is searched by this method. Statement #1 searches an element on the web form with an ID of emailmsg and assigns it to the object called div (it can be any name). Statement #2 sets the content that will be displayed at the location designated by the emailmsg ID to be red.

The hasChildNodes() method in statement #3 checks if a message has already been displayed at the emailmsg ID location. If an error message has already been displayed, it is removed via the removeChild() method in statement #4. The regular expression in statement #5 checks for a valid e-mail address. If the user enters an invalid e-mail address, the appendChild() method is used in statement #6 to display the error message, "Invalid Email" at the emailmsg ID location, as shown in Figure 2-6. The appendChild()

method is for attaching the given node to the document. Remember, a node never appears in the browser window until and unless it is attached to the document using the appendChild( ) method. The child node can be attached to any element.

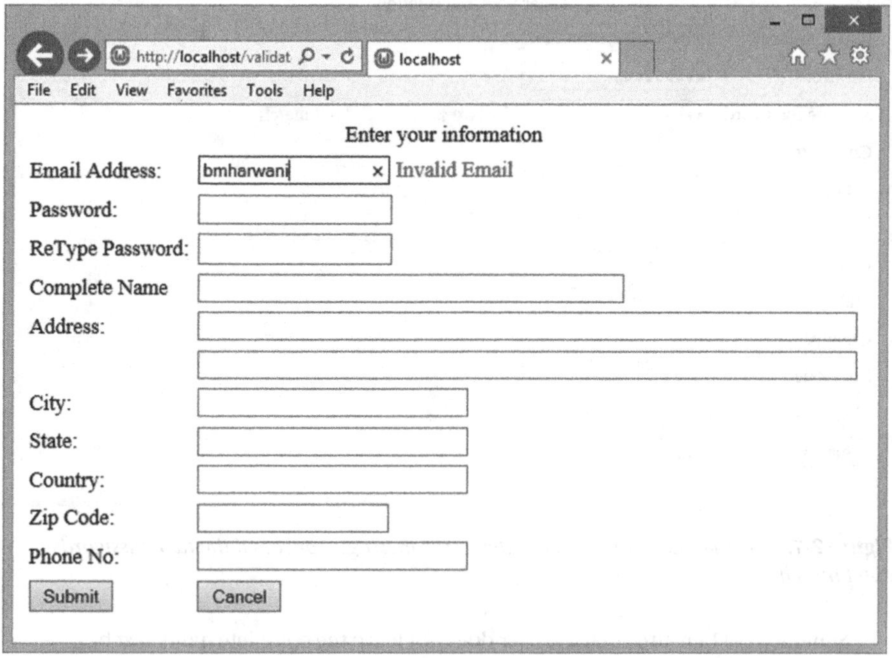

Figure 2-6. *Invalid e-mail error message appears upon entering an invalid email address*

Because an invalid e-mail address has been entered, the user is asked to re-enter it by making the cursor stand at the e-mail address box via the focus() method applied on it through statement #7. Statement #8 returns false so that the form cannot be submitted. The form can be successfully submitted only when the validate() method returns true and that is possible only when data is entered correctly in all the desired fields.

Statement #9 ensures that the length of the password entered is not less than five. Statement #10 ensures that the passwords entered in the Password and ReType Password text boxes are exactly the same. If these passwords don't match, the "The two passwords don't match" error message is displayed at the location that is represented by the repasswdmsg ID (see Figure 2-7).

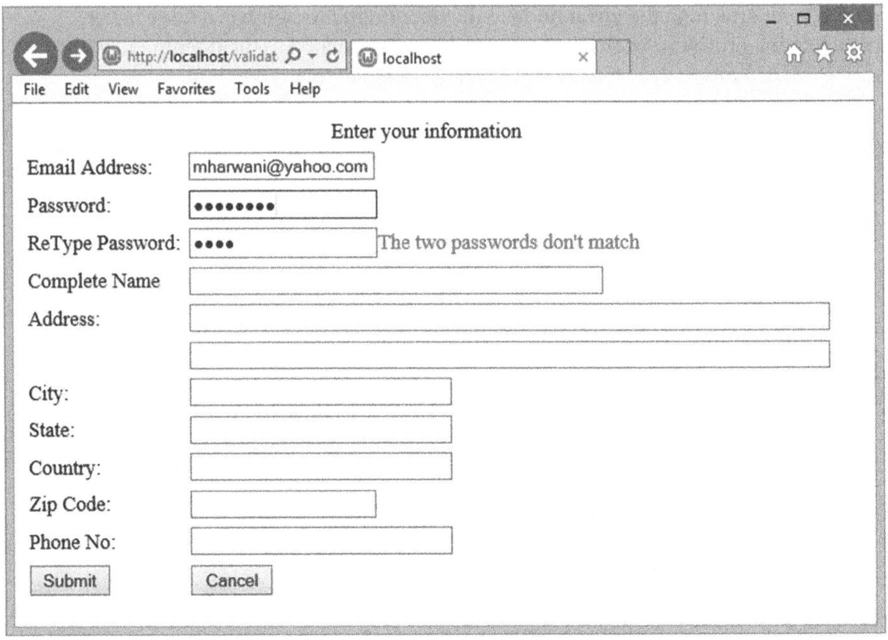

Figure 2-7. The two password don't match error message appears if the two passwords don't match

Statement #11 ensures that the user does not leave the complete name text box blank. If any of the validation checks fail, the validate() method returns false. If the desired text boxes pass through different validation checks successfully, the validation method returns true, consequently the form is submitted and the data entered is transferred to the addcustomer.php script for saving into the database table.

In order to save data into the MySQL server's database table through PHP, you need to understand how the connection is established between PHP and MySQL. You learn how that is done next.

Code for Connecting PHP with MySQL

To connect with a MySQL server, you need to execute the mysqli_connect() method with a valid username and password. The syntax for establishing a connection is:

```
$variable = mysqli_connect("localhost", $user, $password, $database) or die
("Error Message.");
```

■ **Note**   PHP and MySQL version 5 support is no longer bundled with the standard PHP distribution, hence you need to explicitly configure PHP to take advantage of this extension.

50

In the previous syntax, localhost signifies that MySQL server is installed on the local machine but this string is replaced by the IP address of the server or server name in case you are connecting to a remote server. The $user and $password contain the valid user ID and password supplied by the administrator. The variable $database represents the database that you want to connect to and execute the SQL statements on it for inserting or fetching the desired information. The keyword die is for printing error messages if any of the information is wrong. The following example connects the root user to the shopping database:

```
$connect = mysqli_connect("localhost", "root", "gold", "shopping") or die
("Please, check the server connection.");
```

This statement, if successful, returns an object that represents the connection to a MySQL server and the specified database.

Executing SQL Commands Through PHP

After establishing the connection with the database, the next task is to execute the required SQL statement on it. For executing required SQL statements on the database, the mysqli_query method is used with the given syntax:

```
$result = mysqli_query($connect, $sql) or die(mysql_error());
```

The $connect variable represents the connection with the MySQL server and $sql represents the SQL statement that you want to execute on the connected database. The $result variable will store the result of the execution of the SQL statement.

The PHP script shown in Listing 2-12 checks whether the connection with the MySQL server has been established.

Listing 2-12. The checkconnection.php Script Confirms if the Connection with the MySQL Server Is Established

```php
<?php
    // Connect to the database server
    $MySQLi = new MySQLi("localhost", "root", "gold", "shopping");
    if ($MySQLi->errno) {
        printf("Unable to connect to the database:<br /> %s",
        $MySQLi->error);
        exit();
    }
else
    printf("Successfully connected with the MySQL server and shopping
    database is opened");
?>
```

In the previous code, the connection to the MySQL server is established and the shopping database is selected. Upon successful connection, you get the message shown in Figure 2-8.

Figure 2-8. *Message confirms successful connection with the MySQL server and opens the shopping database*

Storing Information in the Database Table

The PHP script for storing a new user's information in the underlying database table is shown in Listing 2-13.

Listing 2-13. The addcustomer.php Script Saves the Customer's Information in the Database Table

```php
<?php
$connect = mysqli_connect("localhost", "root", "gold", "shopping") or die
("Please, check the server connection.");
$email_address = $_POST['emailaddress'];
$password = $_POST['password'];
$repassword = $_POST['repassword'];
$completename = $_POST['complete_name'];
$address1 = $_POST['address1'];
$address2 = $_POST['address2'];
$city = $_POST['city'];
$state = $_POST['state'];
$country = $_POST['country'];
$zipcode = $_POST['zipcode'];
$phone_no = $_POST['phone_no'];

$sql = "INSERT INTO customers (email_address, password, complete_name,
address_line1, address_line2, city, state, zipcode, country, cellphone_no)
VALUES ('$email_address',(PASSWORD('$password')), '$completename', '$address1',
'$address2','$city', '$state', '$zipcode', '$country', '$phone_no')";
$result = mysqli_query($connect, $sql) or die(mysql_error());
```

```
if ($result)
{
?>
    <p>
    Dear, <?php echo $completename; ?> your account is successfully created
<?php
}
else
{
    echo "Some error occurred. Please use different email address";
}
?>
```

This PHP script saves the information entered by the user in the web form that was displayed through the `validatesignup.php` script (refer to Listing 2-10) into the `customers` table of the shopping database. Recall in Chapter 1 that you created the shopping database and the different tables that will be required for this e-commerce site

You can see that first of all, the connection to MySQL server is established and the shopping database is selected. The information of the user-entered `invalidatesignup.php` script is assigned to the $_POST array. The information in the $_POST array is retrieved and stored in different variables. Thereafter, a SQL statement to insert a record in the `customers` table is executed and the users are informed about their successful account creation, as shown in Figure 2-9.

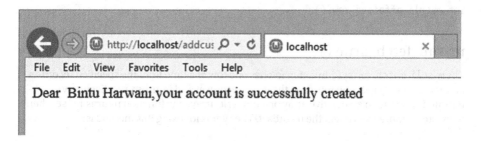

Figure 2-9. *Message confirming successful user account creation*

Accessing Information from the Database

Information that is stored in the database is meant for future use. It means you can access information from the database whenever required. To access information from the database, the following four methods are used:

- `mysqli_num_rows()`—Returns the count of rows in a given recordset.

- `mysqli_affected_rows()`—Returns the count of rows affected by the specified SQL command.

- `mysqli_fetch_array()`—Returns one row at a time from the given recordset.

- `extract()`—Extracts the columns or fields in the specified row.

Let's discuss these methods in detail.

mysqli_num_rows()

The `mysqli_num_rows()` method returns the count of rows that exists in the specified recordset. The syntax for using this method is as follows:

`int mysqli_num_rows(recordset)`

Where `recordset` represents the records or rows that are retrieved upon execution of the SQL SELECT statement through the `mysqli_query()` method.

mysqli_affected_rows()

The `mysql_affected_rows()` method returns the count of the rows that are affected by a DELETE, INSERT, REPLACE, or UPDATE statement executed in the specified SQL query. This method is used immediately after an SQL statement is executed through the `mysqli_query()` method. The syntax for using this method is as follows:

`int mysqli_affected_rows()`

mysqli_fetch_array()

The `mysqli_fetch_array()` function fetches one row at a time from the specified recordset or array of rows. It gets one row from the given recordset and returns `true`. Each row is returned either as an associative array or a numeric array. The function returns `false` when there are no more rows left in the recordset. The syntax for using this method is:

`row=mysqli_fetch_array(recordset,array_type)`

Where the `recordset` represents the rows that are returned upon executing the `mysqli_query()` function.

The `array_type` parameter is optional and it represents the array format in which the fetched row needs to be returned. Available options for this parameter are:

- `MYSQL_ASSOC`—Returns a row in associative array format.

- `MYSQL_NUM`—Returns a row in numeric array format.

- `MYSQL_BOTH`—The default. Returns a row that can be used as both an associative as well as a numeric array. That is, the array returned has both associative and number indices.

After a row is retrieved, the mysqli_fetch_array() function automatically moves to the next row in the recordset. Each subsequent call to this function returns the next row in the specified recordset. For example, the following statement fetches one row from the specified $result i.e. recordset and returns the row in associative array format:

```
$row = mysqli_fetch_array($result, MYSQLI_ASSOC)
```

extract()

The extract() function extracts all the variables or columns stored in the specified array or row. The syntax for using this method is as follows:

```
extract(array/row)
```

For example, this extracts all the columns in the specified row:

```
extract($row);
```

Let's now look at how to apply these methods to authenticate a user.

Implementing Authentication

Authenticating a user means determining whether the visitor is already registered on the e-commerce site or not. Applying authentication is a two-step process:

1. You have already learned to display and execute a script that enables visitors to sign up and create an account on your site. To verify that that the visitor is already registered, they will be provided with a sign-in form that will prompt them to enter a valid e-mail address and password.

2. After entering an e-mail address and password, when the user clicks the Submit button in the sign-in form, they are taken to another script that accesses the customers table and confirms if any customer (row) exists with the supplied e-mail address and password. If a customer exists with the specified e-mail address and password, it means the visitor is already registered to your site and a welcome message will be displayed on the screen. If no row exists in the customers table with the supplied e-mail address and password, it means either the visitor is not registered to your site or has entered the wrong information. Hence, the visitor is provided two links to choose from—one will navigate them to create a new account and the other will allow them to try to sign in again.

The PHP script called signin.php is shown in Listing 2-14. It performs the first step of implementing authentication—displaying the sign-in form.

Listing 2-14. The signin.php Script for Displaying the Sign-In Form

```html
<html>
    <head>
    </head>
    <body>
    <form action="validateuser.php" method="post">
        <table border="0" cellspacing="1" cellpadding="3">
        <tr><td>Email Aaddress:</td><td><input type="text"
        name="emailaddress"></td></tr>
        <tr><td>Password:</td><td><input type="password" name="password">
        </td></tr>
        <tr><td colspan=2 align="center"><input type="submit" name="submit"
        value="Login"></td></tr>
        </table>
    </form>
    </body>
</html>
```

The script displays two text boxes to the visitor, one for entering an e-mail address and other for entering a password (see Figure 2-10). After the user enters an e-mail address and password and clicks Submit, the information entered in the form will be assigned to the $_POST array and sent to the validateuser.php script to check if any user exists in the customers table with the supplied e-mail address and password.

Figure 2-10. Sign-in form prompting the user to enter a valid e-mail address and password

The PHP script called `validateuser.php` is shown in Listing 2-15. It performs the second step of authentication—it verifies whether the information entered by the visitor is valid.

Listing 2-15. The validateuser.php Script for Authenticating the User

```
<html>
<head>
</head>
<body>
<?php
    $connect = mysqli_connect("localhost", "root", "gold", "shopping") or
    die("Please, check your server connection.");
    $query = "SELECT email_address, password, complete_name FROM customers
    WHERE email_address like '" . $_POST['emailaddress'] . "' " .
        "AND password like (PASSWORD('" . $_POST['password'] . "'))";
    $result = mysqli_query($connect, $query) or die(mysql_error());
    if (mysqli_num_rows($result) == 1) {
        while ($row = mysqli_fetch_array($result, MYSQLI_ASSOC)) {
            extract($row);
            echo "Welcome " . $complete_name . " to our Shopping Mall <br>";
        }
    }
    else {
?>
    Invalid Email address and/or Password<br>
    Not registered?
    <a href="validatesignup.php">Click here</a> to register.<br><br><br>
    Want to Try again<br>
    <a href="signin.php">Click here</a> to try login again.<br>
    <?php
        }
?>
</body>
</html>
```

As expected, a connection to MySQL server is established and the shopping database is selected. A SQL statement is written to search in the customers table. The SQL statement checks if there is any row in the customers table whose e-mail address and password matches the e-mail address and passwords in the $_POST array. Recall that the e-mail address and password entered in the form displayed through the signin.php script are assigned to the $_POST array and navigation to the validateuser.php.

If a customer exists in the customers table that matches the supplied e-mail address and password, a welcome message is displayed to the user (see Figure 2-11—bottom).

If no row exists in the `customers` table (that matches the visitor's e-mail address and password), it is assumed that either the visitor is not yet registered or they entered an invalid e-mail address or password. Consequently, two links are displayed to the visitor to choose from—one to create a new account (`validatesignup.php`) and another to try to sign in again (`signin.php`) (see Figure 2-11—top).

Figure 2-11. *Message that appears upon entering an incorrect e-mail address or password (top) and the welcome message displayed upon entering a correct e-mail address and password (bottom)*

Summary

In this chapter, you learned how to write and run your first PHP script. You also saw how information is passed from one script to another. You learned to get information from the user by creating a sign-up form. To store information about the new customer, you learned about the methods that are required in establishing connections between PHP and a MySQL server.

You learned about creating and executing scripts for storing user information in the `customers` table. Finally, you learned about the methods required to access information from the database and used that knowledge to authenticate a user (by creating a sign-in script).

In the next chapter, you will learn how to access the `products` table and display a list of products in it. Also, you will learn to display images of the products. You will learn to implement a search box in the e-commerce site to enable visitors to search the desired products quickly, to remember what visitors like, and finally, you will learn about session handling too.

■ ■ ■

CHAPTER 3

Accessing the Database Using PHP

On an e-commerce site, it is essential to display product information next to its image in as much detail as possible. Because there can be a huge number of products, the information is stored in a database. Recall that you already created a products table that contains several products categorized into different areas. This chapter begins by explaining how product information is accessed from the products table and displayed on the screen.

In this chapter, you are going to learn about the following:

- Accessing products and displaying them on screen

- Creating a drop-down menu

- Displaying products in specific categories

- Adding a web site header

- Implementing a search feature

- Showing product details

- Session handling

- Signing in and out

- Defining a home page for the site

Accessing Products and Displaying Them on Screen

You have already learned about the functions that are used to establish a connection with the MySQL server and to open the database to perform operations. You also learned about the procedure to execute a SQL query on a specified database. The allitemslist.php script, shown in Listing 3-1, uses those functions to access product information from the products table and display them on the screen in a tabular format.

Listing 3-1. The allitemslist.php script for Displaying Items in the products Table

```
<html>
<head>
</head>
<body>
<?php
$connect = mysqli_connect("localhost", "root", "gold", "shopping") or
die("Please, check your server connection.");
$query = "SELECT item_code, item_name, description, imagename, price FROM
products";
$results = mysqli_query($connect, $query) or die(mysql_error());
echo "<table border=\"0\">";
$x=1;
echo "<tr>";
while ($row = mysqli_fetch_array($results, MYSQLI_ASSOC))  {
if ($x <= 3)
{
$x = $x + 1;
extract($row);
echo "<td style=\"padding-right:15px;\">";
echo "<a href=itemdetails.php?itemcode=$item_code>";
echo '<img src=' . $imagename . ' style="max-width:220px;max-height:240px;
width:auto;height:auto;"></img><br/>';
echo $item_name .'<br/>';
echo "</a>";
echo '$'.$price .'<br/>';
echo "</td>";
}
else
{
$x=1;
echo "</tr><tr>";
}
}
echo "</table>";
?>
</body>
</html>
```

This code first connects to the MySQL server as a user root and selects the shopping database. Then, a SQL statement is written to retrieve all the rows from the products table. The SQL query is executed and the rows are fetched from the products table and then assigned to the $results array. After that, with the help of the while loop, one row at a time is fetched from the$results array and the product information is displayed on the screen in the form of a table (see Figure 3-1). Variable x is used to display three products in a row.

Figure 3-1. All items in the products table displayed along with their images

To link to different web pages and enable users to access the required information from the site, you need to create a drop-down menu. Let's see how that is done.

Creating a Drop-Down Menu

Assuming that your site sells electronics, home and furniture products, and books, the drop-down menu needs to provide links to these product sections. Also, assuming that the site sells smart phones, laptops, cameras, and televisions, these product categories must be grouped under the Electronics section. The menu.php file, shown in Listing 3-2, defines a drop-down menu that provides links to these product categories.

Listing 3-2. The menu.php script for displaying a drop-down menu for the e-commerce site

```
<!DOCTYPE html>
<head>
<meta charset="utf-8">
<title>Bintu Online Bazar</title>
<link rel="stylesheet" href="css/style.css">
</head>
```

```
<body>
<div class="container">
<nav>
<ul class="nav">
<li><a href="index.php">Home</a></li>
<li class="dropdown">
<a href="index.php">Electronics</a>
<ul>
<li><a href="itemlist.php?category=CellPhone">Smart Phones</a></li>
<li><a href="itemlist.php?category=Laptop">Laptops</a></li>
<li><a href="index.php">Cameras </a></li>
<li><a href="index.php">Televisions</a></li>
</ul>
</li>
<li class="dropdown">
<a href="index.php">Home & Furniture</a>
<ul class="large">
<li><a href="index.php">Kitchen Essentials</a></li>
<li><a href="index.php">Bath Essentials</a></li>
<li><a href="index.php">Furniture</a></li>
<li><a href="index.php">Dining & Serving</a></li>
<li><a href="index.php">Cookware</a></li>
</ul>
</li>
<li><a href="index.php">Books</a></li>
</ul>
</nav>
</div>
<p>
```

You can see in this code that the drop-down menu is made using the unordered list element. The menu contains four main sections called Home, Electronics, Home & Furniture, and Books. The Electronics menu has four submenu options—Smart Phones, Laptops, Cameras, and Televisions. Similarly, the Home & Furniture menu shows different submenu options. When a product category is chosen via any submenu option, the users will be navigated to the PHP script called itemlist.php. The product category they chose is also sent to the itemlist.php script, which in turn fetches all the products in that category from the database table and displays them on the screen.

To apply foreground and background colors to the drop-down menu and to the menu option when a mouse pointer hovers over it, the script uses a cascading style sheet called style.css. It is linked to the script. Next is a quick introduction to CSS.

CSS

CSS stands for Cascading Style Sheets, which contain different styles, layouts, fonts, and colors for a web site. The advantages of using style sheets are:

- Because all the styles are kept in one place, it is easy to maintain them. To change the style of an element, you don't have to search the entire site. You simply edit it in one place.

- You can change the layout and design of the site very easily.

- Applying styles through CSS makes the code efficient and reduces the website loading time.

Back to the web site, Listing 3-3 shows the styles that are defined in thestyle.css file.

Listing 3-3. The style.css style sheet file applies styles to different HTML elements of the e-commerce site

```css
img {
    max-width:180px;
    max-height:200px;
    width:auto;
    height:auto;
}

ol, ul {
  list-style: none;
}

nav {
  height: 30px;
  border-bottom: 5px solid white;
}

.nav {
  margin: 0 auto;
  width: 600px;
}

.nav a {
  display: block;
  text-decoration: none;
}
```

```css
.nav > li {
  float: left;
  margin-right: 5px;
}

.nav > li > a {
  height: 34px;
  line-height: 34px;
  padding: 0 20px;
  font-weight: bold;
  color: white;
  text-decoration: none;
  border-radius: 3px 3px 0 0;
background-color: blue;
}

.nav > li > a:hover {
  text-decoration: none;
  background: blue;
background-color: navy;
}

.nav > li.active > a, .nav > li > a:active, .nav > .dropdown:hover > a {
  background: white;
  color: blue;
}

.dropdown {
  position: relative;
  border-bottom: 5px solid white;
}

.dropdown:hover ul {
  display: block;
}

.dropdown ul {
  display: none;
  position: absolute;
  top: 39px;
  left: -1px;
  z-index: 20000;
  min-width: 160px;
  padding: 0 0 5px;
  background: blue;
  border: 1px solid #dadada;
```

```css
  border-top: 0;
  border-radius: 0 0 3px 3px;
}

.dropdown ul.large {
  min-width: 200px;
}

.dropdown li {
  display: block;
  margin: 0 18px;
  overflow: visible;
}

.dropdown li + li {
  border-top: 1px solid #eee;
}

.dropdown li a {
  color: #FFF;
  padding: 8px 18px;
  margin: 0 -18px;
}

.dropdown li a:hover {
  background: navy;
}
```

This code gives the drop-down menu a dynamic look. The CSS style shown in Listing 3-3 performs the following tasks:

- Sets the height and width of the images

- Hides the list-item markers (circle, square, etc.) for the ordered and unordered lists

- Sets the height and bottom borders of the drop-down menu

- Sets the width and margins of the drop-down menu

- Removes the default underlines from the hyperlinks displayed in the menu and submenus

- Sets the list items, i.e. the submenu options, to float to the left in the drop-down menu, keeping the margin on the right

- Sets the height, padding of the text (from the boundary of the drop-down), foreground, and background color of the text, and removes the default underlines from the hyperlinks

- Sets the background and foreground color of the text when the mouse hovers over the menu and submenu options

Upon running the menu.php script with the CSS styles in style.css applied to it, you get the drop-down menu shown in Figure 3-2.

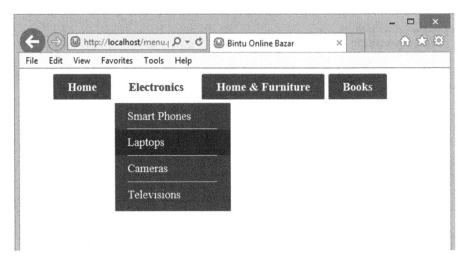

Figure 3-2. *Drop-down menu displaying different product categories*

The allitemslist.php script shown in Listing 3-1 displays all the products defined in the products table. The script works fine, but the users will spend lots of time searching for their desired products from the list. How about displaying only the products of the category selected by the users from the drop-down menu?

The itemlist.php script shown in Listing 3-4 does exactly this. It displays only the products whose category the users chose from the drop-down menu.

Listing 3-4. The itemlist.php script for displaying products whose category is selected from the drop-down menu

```php
<?php
include('menu.php');
$connect = mysqli_connect("localhost", "root", "gold", "shopping") or
die("Please, check your server connection.");
$category=$_REQUEST['category'];
$query = "SELECT item_code, item_name, description, imagename, price FROM
products " .
"where category like '$category' order by item_code";
$results = mysqli_query($connect, $query) or die(mysql_error());
echo "<table border=\"0\">";
$x=1;
echo "<tr>";
```

```
while ($row = mysqli_fetch_array($results, MYSQLI_ASSOC))  {
if ($x <= 3)                                                          // #1
{
$x = $x + 1;
extract($row);
echo "<td style=\"padding-right:15px;\">";
echo "<a href=itemdetails.php?itemcode=$item_code>";                 // #2
echo '<img src=' . $imagename . ' style="max-width:220px;max-height:240px;
width:auto;height:auto;"></img><br/>';
echo $item_name .'<br/>';
echo "</a>";
echo '$'.$price .'<br/>';
echo "</td>";
}
else
{
$x=1;
echo "</tr><tr>";
}
}
echo "</table>";
?>
</body>
</html>
```

At the top of the script, another script called menu.php is included to make the drop-down menu appear in the web site. Recall that the menu.php displays different categories of products. When a user selects a category, navigation takes place to the itemlist.php file and the selected product category is also passed.

The selected product category is accessed through the $_REQUEST array and assigned to the category's variable.

As expected, a connection to the MySQL server is established as the user, root, and the shopping database is selected for performing operations. A SQL query is executed to fetch all the products from the products table that match the category selected by the user. The fetched rows are assigned to the results recordset. From the results recordset, products are assigned one by one and displayed on the screen.

This script is set to display only three products in a line; hence, a variable x is used (see statement #1) that makes only three products appear in a line. You can always change the value of the variable x to display your desired number of products in a row.

The information that is displayed is the product image, its name, and price. To enable users to display detailed product information, a hyperlink is created on the product's image and its name via statement #2. That means that if the user clicks on any product's image or name, navigation will take place to the itemdetails.php script, which will display more details about that product. While navigating to the itemdetails.php script, the code of the selected product is also passed. The itemdetails.php script in turn will use the product code to fetch more information about the product, like its description and features, from the products table. Products are displayed in the format shown in Figure 3-3. You can see that only three products are displayed in a row and hyperlinks are created on the products' images and names.

Figure 3-3. *The web page displaying all the smartphones available for sale on the site*

Upon looking at the output shown in Figure 3-3, you will find something important missing, and that is the web site header. The header not only displays the web site's name and Search box, but it also shows frequently used icons and links.

Adding a Web Site Header

To display the web site header, you'll modify the menu.php script shown in Listing 3-2 to appear as the topmenu.php script shown in Listing 3-5. Only the code in bold is new; the rest of the code is same as you saw in Listing 3-2.

Listing 3-5. The topmenu.php script for displaying headers for the e-commerce site, including the drop-down menu

```
<!DOCTYPE html>
<head>
<meta charset="utf-8">
<title>Bintu Online Bazar</title>
<link rel="stylesheet" href="css/style.css">
</head>
<body>
<table width="100%" cellspacing="0" cellpadding="2">
<col style="width:30%">
<col style="width:40%">
<col style="width:20%">
<tr><td style="background-color:cyan;color:Blue;"></td><td
style="background-color:cyan;color:Blue;"></td><td style="background-
color:cyan;color:Blue;">
<tr><td style="font-size: 35px;color:blue;background-color:cyan;"><!-- #1 -->
<b>Bintu Online Bazar</b></font></td>
<td bgcolor="cyan">
<form  method="post" action="searchitems.php">                 <!-- #2 -->
<input  size="50" type="text" name="tosearch">
<input  type="submit" name="submit" value="Search">
</form></td>
<td bgcolor="cyan" ><a href="cart.php"><img style="max-width:40px;
max-height:40px;width:auto;height:auto;" src="images/cart.png"></img>
<span id="cartcountinfo"></span></a><!-- #3 -->
</td></tr>
</table>
<div class="container">
<nav>
<ul class="nav">
<li><a href="index.php">Home</a></li>
<li class="dropdown">
<a href="index.php">Electronics</a>
<ul>
<li><a href="itemlist.php?category=CellPhone">Smart Phones</a></li>
<li><a href="itemlist.php?category=Laptop">Laptops</a></li>
<li><a href="index.php">Cameras </a></li>
<li><a href="index.php">Televisions</a></li>
</ul>
</li>
```

```
<li class="dropdown">
<a href="index.php">Home & Furniture</a>
<ul class="large">
<li><a href="index.php">Kitchen Essentials</a></li>
<li><a href="index.php">Bath Essentials</a></li>
<li><a href="index.php">Furniture</a></li>
<li><a href="index.php">Dining & Serving</a></li>
<li><a href="index.php">Cookware</a></li>
</ul>
</li>
<li><a href="index.php">Books</a></li>
</ul>
</nav>
</div>
<p>
```

To display a header, a `table` element is defined consisting of three columns. To display the web site title, Search box, and cart icon, the width of the columns is defined in the ratios—30%, 40%, and 20%. The background color of the table is set to cyan and the foreground color is set to blue. To display the web site title, "Bintu Online Bazar," the font size is set to 35px through statement #1. Statement #2 navigates the users to the `searchitems.php` script when they click the Search button. The text entered by the user in the Search box is also passed to the `searchitems.php` script through the `$_POST` array.

Following the Search box, a cart icon is displayed through statement #3. The width and height of the icon is set to 30px. The cart icon, when clicked, will navigate to the `cart.php` script, which in turn displays the information about the products that are selected in the cart. The span ID, `cartcountinfo`, will be used to display the count of the products chosen in the cart.

The `topmenu.php` script, when executed, displays the web site header shown in Figure 3-4.

Figure 3-4. *The header of the web site showing the title, the Search box, and the cart image with the drop-down menu*

Most of your site visitors will not have enough time to view the entire range of products you sell. They simply want to search for their desired product and see its details immediately on the screen. To add such a feature, you have to add a Search box to your site, which you'll learn to do in the next section.

Implementing a Search Feature

Recall that you added a Search box to the web site header. Users can enter text in the Search box and then click the Search button. The entire products table will be searched for the specified text and all the products that contain that text (whether in their name, description, features, and so on) will be displayed on the screen.

The searchitems.php script shown in Listing 3-6 searches the text entered in the Search box in all the columns of the products table. If the text appears in any of the columns, that row will be displayed on the screen.

Listing 3-6. The searchitems.php script displays items that match the text entered in the search box

```php
<?php
include('topmenu.php');
$connect = mysqli_connect("localhost", "root", "gold", "shopping") or
die("Please, check your server connection.");
$tosearch=$_POST['tosearch'];
$query = "select * from products where ";
$query_fields = Array();
$sql = "SHOW COLUMNS FROM products";                                      // #1
$columnlist = mysqli_query($connect, $sql) or die(mysql_error());         // #2
while($arr = mysqli_fetch_array($columnlist, MYSQLI_ASSOC)){              // #3
extract($arr);
$query_fields[] = $Field . " like('%". $tosearch . "%')";
}
$query .= implode(" OR ", $query_fields);
$results = mysqli_query($connect, $query) or die(mysql_error());
echo "<table border=\"0\" >";
$x=1;
echo "<tr>";
while ($row = mysqli_fetch_array($results, MYSQLI_ASSOC)) {
if ($x <= 3)
{
$x = $x + 1;
extract($row);
echo "<td style=\"padding-right:15px;\">";
echo "<a href=itemdetails.php?itemcode=$item_code>";
echo '<img src=' . $imagename . ' style="max-width:220px;max-height:240px;
width:auto;height:auto;"></img><br/>';
echo $item_name .'<br/>';
echo "</a>";
echo '$'.$price .'<br/>';
echo "</td>";
}
```

```
else
{
$x=1;
echo "</tr><tr>";
}
}
echo "</table>";
?>
```

The topmenu.php script is included at the top to display the web site header and the drop-down menu. The code first connects to the MySQL server as a user, root, and the shopping database are selected for performing operations. The text entered by the user in the Search box in the topmenu.php script is accessed and assigned to the tosearch variable.

Because you want to search the text in the tosearch variable in all columns of the products table, all the column names of the products table are accessed (see statement #1) and assigned to the columnlist variable through statement #2. Using a while loop, a SQL query is created that accesses every column of the products table and checks if the desired text is found in it (see statement #3). The SQL query is executed and all the products that contain the searched text in any of the columns are displayed on the screen. For example, if you enter **lenovo** into the Search box, you will get all the products that contain that text, as shown in Figure 3-5.

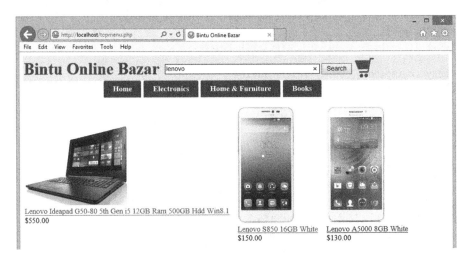

Figure 3-5. *Web page displaying the products that match the text entered in the Search box*

All the scripts that you have created so far in this chapter display the minimum information about the product—the product image, name, and price. What if the user wants to see more details about a product?

Showing Product Details

So, how do you display additional product details, like a description and its different features? Recall from Chapter 1 that all the information about the product—including its code, name, price, description, and so on—is stored in the products table. The product features are stored in a separate table called productfeatures. The itemdetails.php script, shown in Listing 3-7, displays detailed information about the selected product.

Listing 3-7. The itemdetails.php script displays detailed information about the selected item

```php
<?php
include('topmenu.php');
$connect = mysqli_connect("localhost", "root", "gold", "shopping") or
die("Please, check your server connection.");
$code=$_REQUEST['itemcode'];
$query = "SELECT item_code, item_name, description, imagename, price FROM
products " .
"where item_code like '$code'";
$results = mysqli_query($connect, $query) or       die(mysql_error()); // #1
$row = mysqli_fetch_array($results, MYSQLI_ASSOC);
extract($row);
echo "<table width=\"100%\" cellspacing=\"0\" cellpadding=\"5\">";
echo "<tr><td style=\"padding: 3px;\" rowspan=\"6\">";
echo '<img src=' . $imagename . ' style="max-width:200px;max-height:260px;
width:auto;height:auto;"></img></td>';
echo "<td colspan=\"2\" align=\"center\" style=\"font-family:verdana;
font-size:150%;\"><b>";
echo $item_name;
echo "</b></td></tr><tr><td colspan=\"2\"><table><tr><td>";
$itemname=urlencode($item_name);
$itemprice=$price;
$itemdescription=$description;
$pfquery = "SELECT feature1, feature2, feature3, feature4, feature5,
feature6 FROM productfeatures " .
"where item_code like '$code'";                                    // #2
$pfresults = mysqli_query($connect, $pfquery) or die(mysql_error());
$pfrow = mysqli_fetch_array($pfresults, MYSQLI_ASSOC);
extract($pfrow);
echo $feature1;
echo "</td><td>";
echo $feature2;
echo "</td></tr><tr><td>";
echo $feature3;
echo "</td><td>";
echo $feature4;
echo "</td></tr><tr><td>";
```

```
echo $feature5;
echo "</td><td>";
echo $feature6;
echo "</td></tr><tr>";
echo "<form method=\"POST\" action=\"cart.php?action=add&icode=$item_
code&iname=$itemname&iprice=$itemprice\">";
echo "<td colspan=\"2\" style=\"font-family:verdana; font-size:150%;\">";
echo " Quantity: <input type=\"text\" name=\"quantity\" size=\"2\">  
 Price: " . $itemprice;
echo "</td></tr><tr><td  colspan=\"2\"><input type=\"submit\"
name=\"buynow\" value=\"Buy Now\" style=\"font-size:150%;\">";
echo "      <input type=\"submit\"
name=\"addtocart\" value=\"Add To Cart\" style=\"font-size:150%;\"></td>";
echo" </form>";
echo "</tr></table></table>";
echo "<p  style=\"font-size:140%;\">Description</p>";
echo $itemdescription;
?>
```

After establishing a connection with the SQL server and selecting the shopping database, the product code sent by the itemlist.php and searchitems.php scripts is accessed and assigned to the code variables. Recall that the itemlist.php and searchitems.php scripts display the products list consisting of the product's image, its name, and its price. When a user clicks on any product's image or name, the user is navigated to the itemdetails.php script and the code of the selected product is sent to the script.

Statement #1 executes the SQL command that accesses the item name, description, image name, and price of the product that matches the product code.

The fetched product information is displayed on the screen. Besides the product's description and price, you want to display its features too. So, statement #2 defines a SQL statement that accesses the feature1, feature2, etc. columns from the productfeatures table. The SQL statement is executed and the features of the product are displayed on the screen.

Below the product features, a text box is provided so users can enter the required quantity of the product being displayed. The quantity entered by the user is assigned to the quantity variable and is sent to the cart.php script along with the item_code, item_name, and price of the item when the user presses the Add to Cart button.

The itemdetails.php script is executed from the itemlist.php and searchitems.php scripts when any product image or its name is clicked. Upon clicking on any product image or name, its detailed information will be displayed, as shown in Figure 3-6.

Figure 3-6. *Web page displaying the detailed information of the selected product*

After learning the technique for displaying products and their information, you're ready to learn how a web site can remember user information.

Session Handling

Because HTTP is a stateless protocol, the interaction between browsers and web servers is *stateless*. This means that each HTTP request that a browser sends to a web server is independent of any other request. The stateless nature of HTTP allows users to browse the web by following hypertext links and visiting pages in any order. HTTP also allows applications to distribute or even replicate content across multiple servers to balance the load generated by a high number of requests. These features are possible because of the stateless nature of HTTP.

The drawback of HTTP being stateless is that a web page does not remember the user's information. If the user inserts some information on one web page and moves to another page, that data will be lost. For example, if the user has signed in through a sign-in page, the moment the user clicks on some link and navigates to another page, that information is lost. In order to remember certain data between web pages, like the items that are selected in the cart by a particular user, sites must use session handling. The session enables storing of user information in the server's memory. It can store any type of object along with the custom objects. Session data is stored separately for every client.

Because HTTP is a stateless protocol, to keep track of the user, the session ID needs to be continually correlated with the user. This correlation is done through the following methods:

- **Cookies**—When the client connects to the server for the first time, the server drops the cookies on the client's machine. In every subsequent request, the server uses the cookies to recognize the user and his settings.

- **URL Rewriting**—The session ID is often appended to the query string of the URL, as shown in this example:

  ```
  http://www.bmharwani.com/productdetails.php;
  jsessionid=2243781FG55544K1
  ```

- **Hidden fields**—A hidden field is embedded into the session ID within a web form. The session ID is extracted from the hidden field to recognize the user.

Let's take a quick look at the different functions that are required in session handling.

Functions Used in Session Handling

A *session* is a combination of a server-side file containing all the data you want to store and a client-side cookie containing a reference to the server data. The file and the client-side cookie are created using the session_start() function, as explained next.

session_start()

The session_start() function initializes the session data. It creates a session or resumes the current one based on the current session ID. The syntax for using this function is:
bool session_start (void)
This function always returns true. If you want to use a named session, you must call the session_name()function before calling session_start().
When session_start() is called, PHP checks to see whether the visitor sent a session cookie. If it did, PHP loads the session data. Otherwise, PHP creates a new session file on the server and sends an ID back to the visitor to associate the visitor with the new file. Because each visitor has her own data locked away in a unique session file, you need to call session_start() every time before you try to read session variables. As session_start() needs to send the reference cookie to the user's computer, you write this statement before the body of the web page—even before any spaces.

session_id()

The session_id() function gets or sets the session ID for the current session. More precisely, the session_id() function returns either the session ID for the current session or an empty string ("") if there is no current session (no current session ID exists). The syntax is as follows:

```
string session_id ([ string $id ] )
```

When the id parameter is not supplied, the function returns the session ID of the current session. If the id parameter is supplied, the function replaces the current session with the session whose ID is given. In that case, the session_id() function must be called before session_start() is invoked.

isset()

The isset() function determines whether a variable is set, i.e., whether it is assigned some value or is NULL. The syntax is as follows:

```
bool isset ( variable/variable list)
```

The function returns true if the mentioned variable(s) is set. If the mentioned variable is already unset by the invokingunset() function or is set to NULL, the isset() function will return false.

If multiple parameters are supplied, then isset() will return true only if all of the parameters are set. Evaluation goes from left to right and stops as soon as an unset variable is encountered.

The PHP script called sessionscript1.php is shown in Listing 3-8. It shows how a session is started and how certain variables are set.

Listing 3-8. The sessionscript1.php script set svalues in session variables

```php
<?php
if (session_status() == PHP_SESSION_NONE) {                        // #1
session_start();
}
?>
<!DOCTYPE html>
<html>
<body>
<?php
$_SESSION["username"] = "John";                                    // #2
$_SESSION["cartquantity"] = 3;
$_SESSION["cartprice"] = 19.99;
?>
```

```
Finished with shopping? <br>
Click <a href="sessionscript2.php"> View Cart </a> link to view the quantity
and amount of the products selected in the cart
</body>
</html>
```

Statement #1 ensures that if the session is not yet started, it invokes the session_start() function to create a new session. Statement #2 sets the username variable to the value John. Similarly, the following two statements set the cartquantity and cartprice variables to 3 and 19.99, respectively.

After setting the session variables, the script shows a hyperlink called View Cart, which will navigate the user to another script, calledsessionscript2.php. As expected, the sessionscript2.php script will access values from the session variables and display them on the screen. Upon running this script, the View Cart hyperlink is displayed along with a message, as shown in Figure 3-7.

■ **Note**   The session information can even be stored permanently in a database if required.

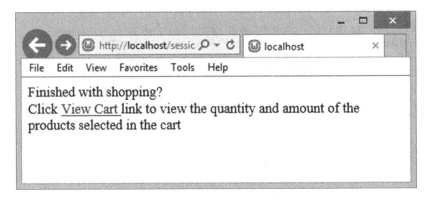

Figure 3-7. *The values of the session variables are set and a link is displayed to access and view the session variables*

The sessionscript2.php script shown in Listing 3-9 completes the following tasks:

- Checks whether a session exists. If not, it starts a new session.

- Checks if the username variable is set and displays a welcome message.

- Retrieves the values in the session variables, cartquantity and cartprice, which were set in the sessionscript1.php script, and displays them on the screen.

Listing 3-9. The sessionscript2.php script retrieves values from the session variables

```php
<?php
if (session_status() == PHP_SESSION_NONE) {
session_start();
}
?>
<html>
<body>
<?php
if (isset($_SESSION['username']))
$username=$_SESSION["username"];
else
$username="Sir/Ma'm";
$cartquantity=$_SESSION["cartquantity"];
$cartprice=$_SESSION["cartprice"];
echo "Session is On and the session id is " . session_id() . "<br>";
echo "Welcome $username. <br>";
echo "There are $cartquantity products chosen in the cart worth
$$cartprice";
?>
</body>
</html>
```

When the script runs, the session ID is displayed along with a welcome message to the user. Also, the cart quantity and cart price are displayed, as shown in Figure 3-8.

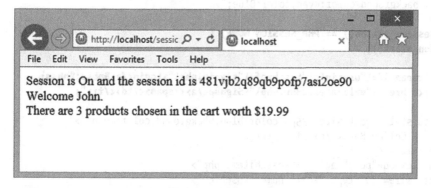

Figure 3-8. The web page displaying the session ID, user name, cart quantity, and price

How about adding the user's sign-in information to the header of the site, displayed through the topmenu.php script shown in Listing 3-5?

81

You can display the Login and Signup links in the header, and they will complete the following tasks:

- Display the username of the user who is signed in or display the Login link that will enable a user to sign in.

- Display the Signup link, which will display a form that enables the user to register on your site.

To do these tasks, modify the topmenu.php script to appear as shown in Listing 3-10. Only the code in bold is new; the rest is the same as shown in Listing 3-5.

Listing 3-10. The topmenu.php header file of the e-commerce site, modified to display signed-in user information

```
<!DOCTYPE html>
<head>
<meta charset="utf-8">
<title>Bintu Online Bazar</title>
<link rel="stylesheet" href="css/style.css">
</head>
<body>
<table  width="100%" cellspacing="0" cellpadding="2">
<col style="width:30%">
<col style="width:40%">
<col style="width:20%">
<tr><td style="background-color:cyan;color:Blue;"></td><td
style="background-color:cyan;color:Blue;"></td><td
style="background-color:cyan;color:Blue;">
<?php
if (session_status() == PHP_SESSION_NONE) {
session_start();
}
echo "<span id=\"userinfo\"><a href=\"signin.php\">Login</a>  
 <a href=\"validatesignup.php\">Signup</a></span></td></tr>";
?>
<tr><td style="font-size: 35px;color:blue;background-color:cyan;">
<b>Bintu Online Bazar</b></font></td>
<td bgcolor="cyan">
<form  method="post" action="searchitems.php">
<input  size="50" type="text" name="tosearch">
<input  type="submit" name="submit" value="Search">
</form></td>
<td bgcolor="cyan" ><a href="cart.php"><img style="max-width:40px;
max-height:40px;width:auto;height:auto;" src="images/cart4.png"></img>
<span id="cartcountinfo"></span></a></td></tr>
</table>
<div class="container">
<nav>
```

```
<ul class="nav">
<li><a href="index.php">Home</a></li>
<li class="dropdown"><a href="index.php">Electronics</a>
<ul>
<li><a href="itemlist.php?category=CellPhone">Smart Phones</a></li>
<li><a href="itemlist.php?category=Laptop">Laptops</a></li>
<li><a href="index.php">Cameras </a></li>
<li><a href="index.php">Televisions</a></li>
</ul>
</li>
<li class="dropdown">
<a href="index.php">Home & Furniture</a>
<ul class="large">
<li><a href="index.php">Kitchen Essentials</a></li>
<li><a href="index.php">Bath Essentials</a></li>
<li><a href="index.php">Furniture</a></li>
<li><a href="index.php">Dining & Serving</a></li>
<li><a href="index.php">Cookware</a></li>
</ul>
</li>
<li><a href="index.php">Books</a></li>
</ul>
</nav>
</div>
<p>
```

The code in bold starts a session. Thereafter, it adds a span with the ID userinfo to the header. The span displays two hyperlinks—Login and Signup (see Figure 3-9). The Login hyperlink will navigate users to the signin.php script, which in turn will display a form prompting the user to enter credential information to sign in to your site. The Signup link will navigate the user to the validatesignup.php script, which displays a form that enables the user to register to your site.

Figure 3-9. The header modified to display the Login and Signup links, which enable visitors to signup and signin to the site

Signing In and Out

Obviously, it's beneficial to store information about your regular customers. Doing so will relieve them from having to enter their addresses, contact information, and so on every time they buy a product from your site. To store information about your frequent customers, you need to enable them to register at your site. The registered customers can sign in any time by entering their e-mail addresses and passwords. When users have completed a purchase, they can then log out from your site. In this section, you'll learn how visitors to your site can be allowed to sign in and sign out.

■ **Note**　The session usually sets a user key on the user's computer, which looks like a long string of chars like `234hjg5hg34g5hj23g532hjg34hjg5k4`. When a session is opened on another page for instance, it will scan the computer for a user key. If there is a match, it will access that session; if not, it will start a new session.

The `signin.php` script shown in Listing 3-11 prompts the users to enter credential information so that they can sign in to your site.

Listing 3-11. The signin.php script displays a sign-in page along with the header and drop-down menu

```
<?php
include('topmenu.php');
?>
<html>
<head>
</head>
<body>
<form action="validateuser.php" method="post">
<table border="0" cellspacing="1" cellpadding="3">
<tr><td>Email Aaddress:</td><td><input type="text" name="emailaddress">
</td></tr>
<tr><td>Password:</td><td><input type="password" name="password"></td></tr>
<tr><td colspan=2 align="center"><input type="submit" name="submit"
value="Login"></td></tr>
</table>
</form>
</body>
</html>
```

The code displays a form that displays two input boxes for the users to enter their e-mail addresses and passwords. The form also shows a button that can be clicked after entering the e-mail address and password. Clicking the button will navigate the users to the `validateuser.php` script. Because the form will be submitted through the HTTP

POST method, the e-mail address and password entered in this form can be accessed in the `validateuser.php` script through the `$_POST` array.

Upon running the script, you get a screen prompting the user to enter an e-mail address and password, as shown in Figure 3-10.

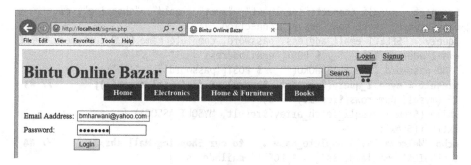

Figure 3-10. *The sign-in web page along with the header and drop-down menu*

After a user enters an e-mail address and password, the next task is to confirm if the information entered is valid. The `validateuser.php` script shown in Listing 3-12 does the following tasks:

- It validates the user, i.e., it determines whether the user has entered a valid e-mail address and password.

- It displays a welcome message if the user is authenticated.

- If an invalid e-mail address or password is entered, it displays an error message followed by two links that enable the users to enter their credentials again or create a new account.

- If the user is authenticated successfully, it updates the header of the site, replacing the Login link with the name of the user along with the welcome message. Also, the Signup link is replaced with the Log Out link.

Listing 3-12. The validateuser.php script displays information about the signed-in user in the site's header

```
<html>
<head>
<script language="JavaScript" type="text/JavaScript">
function updateUser(username){                            // #1
var ajaxUser = document.getElementById("userinfo");      // #2
ajaxUser.innerHTML = "Welcome " + username + "   
<a href=\"logout.php\">Log Out</a>";
}
</script>
</head>
```

```php
<body>
<?php
include('topmenu.php');
if (session_status() == PHP_SESSION_NONE) {
session_start();
}
$connect = mysqli_connect("localhost", "root", "gold", "shopping") or
die("Please, check your server connection.");
$query = "SELECT email_address, password, complete_name FROM customers WHERE
email_address like '" . $_POST['emailaddress'] . "' " .
"AND password like (PASSWORD('" . $_POST['password'] . "'))";
$result = mysqli_query($connect, $query) or die(mysql_error());          // #3
if (mysqli_num_rows($result) == 1) {
while ($row = mysqli_fetch_array($result, MYSQLI_ASSOC)) {
extract($row);
echo "Welcome " . $complete_name . " to our Shopping Mall <br>";          // #4
$_SESSION['emailaddress'] = $_POST['emailaddress'];
$_SESSION['password'] = $_POST['password'];
echo "<SCRIPT LANGUAGE=\"JavaScript\">updateUser('$complete_name');
</SCRIPT>";                                                                // #5
}
}
else {
?>
Invalid Email address and/or Password<br>                                  // #6
Not registered?
<a href="validatesignup.php">Click here</a> to register.<br><br><br>
Want to Try again<br>
<a href="signin.php">Click here</a> to try login again.<br>
<?php
}
?>
</body>
</html>
```

In this code, statement #1 defines a JavaScript function called updateUser that is invoked when users enter a valid e-mail address and password. Statement #2 displays a welcome message along with the user's name in the span ID called userinfo. It also displays a link, called Log Out, which navigates the users to the logout.php script and enables them to log out of your site.

Statement #3 executes a SQL query that determines whether any row exists in the customers table that contains the e-mail address and password that was entered by the user in the signin.php script. Statement #4 displays a welcome message along with the user's name if such a row exists.

Statement #5 invokes the JavaScript function, updateUser, to display a welcome message in the header of the site. Statement #6 and on display an error message and links that enable the user to try to sign in again or create a new account.

If users enter an e-mail address or password that the site doesn't recognize, two links will be displayed on the screen. These links enable users to try to sign in again or create a new account, as shown in Figure 3-11.

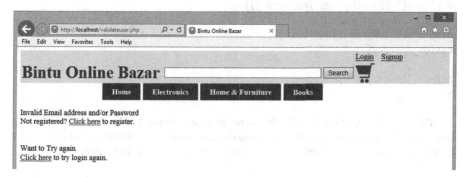

Figure 3-11. *Messages that appear when users enter an unknown e-mail address or password*

If users enter a valid e-mail address and password, a welcome message will be displayed along with their name. This is displayed in the body of the site as well as in the header, as shown in Figure 3-12.

Figure 3-12. *Welcome message displayed when users enter an existing e-mail address and password*

The logout.php script shown in Listing 3-13 destroys the user's session, which then enables them to log out.

The following two methods are used in this script:

- unset()—Unsets or destroys the specified session variable.

- session_destroy()—Destroys all the data associated with the current session. That is, all global and local session variables are destroyed.

87

Listing 3-13. The logout.php script that destroys users' sessions so they can log out

```php
<?php
session_start();
if (isset($_SESSION['emailaddress']))
{
unset($_SESSION['emailaddress']);
session_destroy();
}
include("index.php");
?>
```

The script checks if the e-mail address session variable is set. If it is set, it is destroyed. Also, any data associated with the current session is destroyed. After destroying all the session information, the home page, index.php, is opened.

Defining the Home Page of the Site

The home page is the introductory page of the site and it plays a major role in attracting visitors.

The home page of this e-commerce site displays the site header, a drop-down menu, and images of some of the products that the site sells. The product images being displayed will fade out after a few seconds and will be replaced with others. The process continues to display different images. Upon clicking any image, users will be navigated to the page that shows the complete list of that type of product. For example, when users click on any laptop image, they will be navigated to the page that shows the complete list of all the laptops that are available for sale.

The index.php script shown in Listing 3-14 displays the home page. It contains the site header, a drop-down menu, and three product images that are continuously replaced with other images.

Listing 3-14. The index.php scriptis the home page of the site

```php
<?php
        include('topmenu.php');
?>
<span id="crossfade">
        <a href="itemlist.php?category=CellPhone">
        <img class="bottom" src="images/AppleiPhone4s.jpg"
        style="max-width:350px;max-height:350px;width:auto; height:auto;" />
        <img  class="top" src="images/MicromaxKnight2E471.jpg"
        style="max-width:350px;max-height:350px;width: auto;height: auto;" /></a>
</span>
<span id="crossfade">
        <a href="itemlist.php?category=CellPhone">
        <img class="bottom" src="images/MicrosoftLumia640XL.jpg"
        style="max-width:350px;max-height:350px;width:auto; height: auto;" />
```

```
        <img  class="top" src="images/XperiaT3White.jpg"
        style="max-width:350px;max-height:350px;width:auto;height: auto;" /></a>
</span>
<span id="crossfade">
        <a href="itemlist.php?category=Laptop">
        <img class="bottom" src="images/DellVostro153558.jpg"
        style="max-width:350px;max-height:350px;width:auto;height: auto;" />
        <img  class="top" src="images/HPProbook6570.jpg"
        style="max-width:350px;max-height:350px;width:auto;height: auto;" /></a>
</span>
</body>
</html>
```

In this code, you can see that images of the Apple iPhone 4s smart phone, the Micromax Knight 2E471 smart phone, and the Microsoft Lumia laptop are displayed initially. After a couple of seconds, when these product images fade, images of the Xperia T3 white smart phone, Dell Vostro1, and HP Probook 6570 laptop appear.

The code shown in Listing 3-15 implements the cross-fading technique shown on the home page.

Listing 3-15. The code that implements the cross-fading technique

```
#crossfade {
        position:relative;
        height:350px;
        width:350px;
        margin-right:250px;
}

#crossfade img {
        position:absolute;
        left:0;
        -webkit-transition: opacity 1s ease-in-out;
        -moz-transition: opacity 1s ease-in-out;
        -o-transition: opacity 1s ease-in-out;
        transition: opacity 1s ease-in-out;
}

@keyframes crossfadeFadeInOut {
        0% {
                opacity:1;
        }
        45% {
                opacity:1;
        }
        55% {
                opacity:0;
        }
```

```
        100% {
                opacity:0;
        }
}

#crossfade img.top {
        animation-name: crossfadeFadeInOut;
        animation-timing-function: ease-in-out;
        animation-iteration-count: infinite;
        animation-duration: 5s;
        animation-direction: alternate;
}
```

This code fades the current images after five seconds and makes the next three images visible. This process continues looping. When you run the site, you get the home page shown in Figure 3-13.

Figure 3-13. *The home page of the site showing the site's header, the drop-down menu, and three images*

After a couple of seconds, the current product images fade out and the other product images become visible, as shown in Figure 3-14.

Figure 3-14. *The images on the home page fade out and are replaced with three new images*

Summary

In this chapter, you learned to access products from the products table and display them on the screen in tabular format. You also learned to create a drop-down menu that shows different product categories and implements navigation from one page to another. You also learned to display products that belong to a specific category, define a web site header, implement a search feature, and display detailed information about the selected product. You also learned how a web site remembers information about a visitor via session handling. You learned to apply sign in and sign out features to your site before coding the site's home page.

The next chapter focuses on the items that users choose to place in their carts. You will learn to display the cart and edit the items in the cart. You will also learn how a purchase order is placed and how the user's shipping information is entered and saved. Finally, you will learn to provide different payment modes that users can use to purchase your product(s).

■ ■ ■

CHAPTER 4

Managing the Shopping Cart

Up until now, you have been focusing on displaying the products' listings and their detailed information. In this chapter, you will enable the users to choose the product(s) they want to purchase and add them to the shopping cart.

As the name suggests, a shopping cart is a software module that shows the products chosen by the visitor for purchase. The items in the cart can be revised if required, i.e., after adding the products to the cart, users can remove them from the cart, add more items to the cart, and increase the quantity of the products already selected in the cart. A cart is a database table that temporarily keeps the user's items selected for purchase.

To store and manage items in the cart, a database table called cart was created with the structure defined in Chapter 1. Here, you'll learn to write code to save items to the cart that the visitor wants to buy.

In this chapter, you are going to learn about the following:

- Saving selections to the cart

- Maintaining the cart

- Displaying the cart count in the site header using AJAX

- Proceeding to check out

- Supplying shipping information

- Understanding different payment modes

- Making payments

Saving Selections in the Cart

Recall from Chapter 3 that the itemdetails.php script shown in Listing 3-7 displays the detailed information about the selected product and shows the following two buttons beneath the information:

- Buy Now—Adds the item to the cart and proceeds to checkout.

- Add To Cart—Adds the item to the cart and remains there, thus enabling the user to choose more products.

The Add To Cart button navigates to the cart.php script, which saves the current product's information in the cart table. The code in the cart.php script is shown in Listing 4-1.

Listing 4-1. The cart.php Script Saves the Items Selected by the User

```php
<?php
include('topmenu.php');
if (session_status() == PHP_SESSION_NONE) {
session_start();
}
$connect = mysqli_connect("localhost", "root", "gold", "shopping") or
die("Please, check your server connection.");
$message = "";
$quantity="";
$action="";
$query="";
if (isset($_POST['quantity'])) {
$quantity = trim($_POST['quantity']);
}
if ($quantity=='')
{
$quantity=1;
}
if($quantity <=0)
{
echo "Quantity value is invalid ";
echo "Go Back and enter a valid value";
}
else
{
if (isset($_REQUEST['icode'])) {
$itemcode = $_REQUEST['icode'];
}
if (isset($_REQUEST['iname'])) {
$item_name = $_REQUEST['iname'];
}
if (isset($_REQUEST['iprice'])) {
$price = $_REQUEST['iprice'];
}
if (isset($_POST['modified_quantity'])) {
$modified_quantity = $_POST['modified_quantity'];
}
$sess = session_id();
if (isset($_REQUEST['action'])) {
$action = $_REQUEST['action'];
}
```

```php
switch ($action) {
case "add":
$query="select * from cart where cart_sess = '$sess' and cart_itemcode like
'$itemcode'";
$result = mysqli_query($connect, $query) or die(mysql_error());
if(mysqli_num_rows($result)==1)
{
$row=mysqli_fetch_array($result, MYSQLI_ASSOC);
$qt=$row['cart_quantity'];
$qt=$qt + $quantity;
$query="UPDATE cart set cart_quantity=$qt where cart_sess = '$sess' and
cart_itemcode like '$itemcode'";
$result = mysqli_query($connect, $query)  or die(mysql_error());
}
else
{
$query = "INSERT INTO cart (cart_sess, cart_quantity, cart_itemcode,
cart_item_name, cart_price) VALUES ('$sess', $quantity, '$itemcode',
'$item_name', $price)";
$message = "<div align=\"center\"><strong>Item added.</strong></div>";
}
break;

case "change":
if($modified_quantity==0)
{
$query = "DELETE FROM cart WHERE cart_sess = '$sess' and cart_itemcode like
'$itemcode'";
$message = "<div style=\"width:200px; margin:auto;\">Item deleted</div>";
}
else
{
if($modified_quantity <0)
{
echo "Invalid quantity entered";
}
else
{
$query = "UPDATE cart SET cart_quantity = $modified_quantity  WHERE
cart_sess = '$sess' and cart_itemcode like '$itemcode'";
$message = "<div style=\"width:200px; margin:auto;\">
Quantity changed</div>";
}
}
break;
case "delete":
$query = "DELETE FROM cart WHERE cart_sess = '$sess' and cart_itemcode like
'$itemcode'";
```

```
$message = "<div style=\"width:200px; margin:auto;\">Item deleted</div>";
break;
case "empty":
$query = "DELETE FROM cart WHERE cart_sess = '$sess'";
break;
}
if($query !="")
{
$results = mysqli_query($connect, $query) or die(mysql_error());
echo $message;
}
include("showcart.php");
echo "<SCRIPT LANGUAGE=\"JavaScript\">updateCart();</SCRIPT>";
}
?>
```

The program begins by starting the session. The session ID will be used to remember the items selected in the cart by the particular user. Remember that the status of the session is equal to PHP_SESSION_NONE if the session is enabled and none exists. Then, a connection to the MySQL server is established and the shopping database file is selected. The quantity of the item purchased (stored in the quantity variable) is retrieved from the $_POST array. If the user has not specified a quantity, the default is one. It also verifies that the value of the quantity entered is a non-negative number. The item code, item name, and price (stored in the icode, iname, and iprice variables) sent from the itemdetails. php script are retrieved using the $_REQUEST array and are assigned to the $itemcode, $item_name, and $price variables.

A session is generated and stored in the $sess variable. This session ID is assigned to all the products selected in the cart to identify the items selected by a particular user. The value of the action variable is retrieved and determines the kind of operation to be applied to the cart items. The value of the action variable can be add, change, or delete. When the action variable's value is add, it means the product has to be added to the cart table. Similarly, if the action's value is change, it means a product that is already in the cart needs to be modified, and the delete action means that the specified product has to be deleted from the cart.

When the action variable is add, it is first checked to determine whether the product is already in the cart. If the product is already in the cart, only the quantity field is modified, i.e., the quantity of the product is incremented to indicate the addition. If the product does not exist in the cart, a new row is added to the cart table.

■ **Note** A session is a combination of a server-side file containing all the data you want to store about the visitor and a client-side cookie containing a reference to the server data. The file and the client-side cookie are created using the function session_start(). As you learned in Chapter 3, HTTP is a stateless protocol, which means the session ID must be continuously correlated with the user through the use of cookies, URL rewrites, or hidden fields.

Upon running the script, you get the detailed information of the selected product. You'll also see prompts to enter the quantity of that product, followed by clicking Add To Cart or Buy Now, as shown in Figure 4-1.

Figure 4-1. *Adding the selected item to the cart*

The cart.php script shown in Listing 4-1 is primarily focused on adding products to the cart. After adding products to the cart, you need to maintain it. That is, you need to modify the cart's content based on the visitor's changes. You'll see how that is done in the next section.

Maintaining the Cart

After adding products to the cart, you need a script to display all the products selected in the cart and modify the cart content if required. The showcart.php script shown in Listing 4-2 does the task of displaying items selected in the cart and managing them.

Listing 4-2. The showcart.php Script Displays the Content in the Cart Table and Maintains It

```php
<?php
if ( ! isset($totalamount)) {
$totalamount=0;
}
$totalquantity=0;
if (!session_id()) {
session_start();
}
```

```php
$connect = mysqli_connect("localhost", "root", "gold", "shopping") or
die("Please, check your server connection.");
$sessid = session_id();
$query = "SELECT * FROM cart WHERE cart_sess = '$sessid'";
$results = mysqli_query($connect, $query) or die (mysql_query());
if(mysqli_num_rows($results)==0)
{
echo "<div style=\"width:200px; margin:auto;\">Your Cart is empty</div> ";
}
else
{
?>
<table border="1" align="center" cellpadding="5">
<tr><td> Item Code</td><td>Quantity</td><td>Item Name</td><td>Price</
td><td>Total Price</td>
<?php
while ($row = mysqli_fetch_array($results, MYSQLI_ASSOC)) {
extract($row);
echo "<tr><td>";
echo $cart_itemcode;
echo "</td>";
echo "<td><form method=\"POST\" action=\"cart.php?action=change&icode=
$cart_itemcode\"><input type=\"text\" name=\"modified_quantity\" size=\"2\"
value=\"$cart_quantity\">";
echo "</td><td>";
echo $cart_item_name;
echo "</td><td>";
echo $cart_price;
echo "</td><td>";
$totalquantity = $totalquantity + $cart_quantity;
$totalprice = number_format($cart_price * $cart_quantity, 2);
$totalamount=$totalamount + ($cart_price * $cart_quantity);
echo $totalprice;
echo "</td><td>";
echo "<input type=\"submit\" name=\"Submit\"  value=\"Change quantity\">
</form></td>";
echo "<td>";
echo "<form method=\"POST\" action=\"cart.php?action=delete&icode=$cart_
itemcode\">";
echo "<input type=\"submit\" name=\"Submit\" value=\"Delete Item\"></form>
</td></tr>";
}
echo "<tr><td >Total</td><td>$totalquantity</td><td></td><td></td><td>";
$totalamount = number_format($totalamount, 2);
echo $totalamount;
echo "</td></tr>";
echo "</table><br>";
```

```
echo "<div style=\"width:400px; margin:auto;\">You currently have " .
$totalquantity . " product(s) selected in your cart</div> ";
?>
<table border="0" style="margin:auto;">
<tr><td   style="padding: 10px;">
<form method="POST" action="cart.php?action=empty">
<input type="submit" name="Submit" value="Empty Cart"
style="font-family:verdana; font-size:150%;" >
</form>
</td><td>
<form method="POST" action="checklogin.php">
<input id="cartamount" name="cartamount" type="hidden" value= "<?php echo
$totalamount ; ?>">
<input type="submit" name="Submit" value="Checkout"
style="font-family:verdana; font-size:150%;" >
</form>
</td></tr></table>
<?php
}
?>
</body>
</html>
```

The program determines whether the session ID is already set. If not, a new session is started. As you read earlier, the session ID helps to identify the products selected by the specific visitor of the site. Thereafter, a connection to the MySQL server is established and the shopping database is selected. A SQL query is executed to check if there are any products in the cart with the given session ID. If there are, that means the visitor has added one or more products to the cart already. In that case, all the items stored in the cart, along with their respective quantities, are displayed on the screen.

If no products are found in the cart table that match the given session ID, it means no products are in the cart. A message is displayed on the screen indicating that the visitor has "0 products selected in the cart".

The script enables the visitor to perform the following tasks:

- Add more products to the cart by selecting any category of item from the top menu.

- Modify the quantity of any item already in the cart.

- Delete an item from the cart or empty the cart entirely.

Upon running the script, you see the products selected in the cart, as shown in Figure 4-2. Note that only one product is selected in the cart at this point.

99

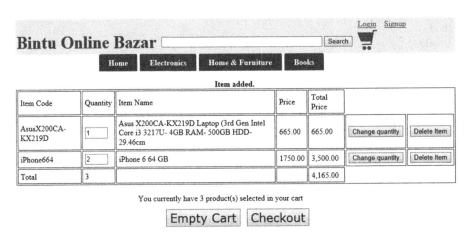

Figure 4-2. *Maintaining the cart*

Assuming the visitor added two iPhone smartphones to the cart, the cart's content would now appear as shown in Figure 4-3.

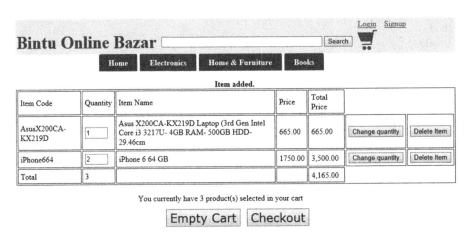

Figure 4-3. *Showing items selected in the cart*

You can always change the quantity of any product by entering the desired quantity in the textbox, followed by clicking the Change Quantity button found in the product's row. Upon changing the quantity of the iPhone product to 1, the cart will appear as shown in Figure 4-4.

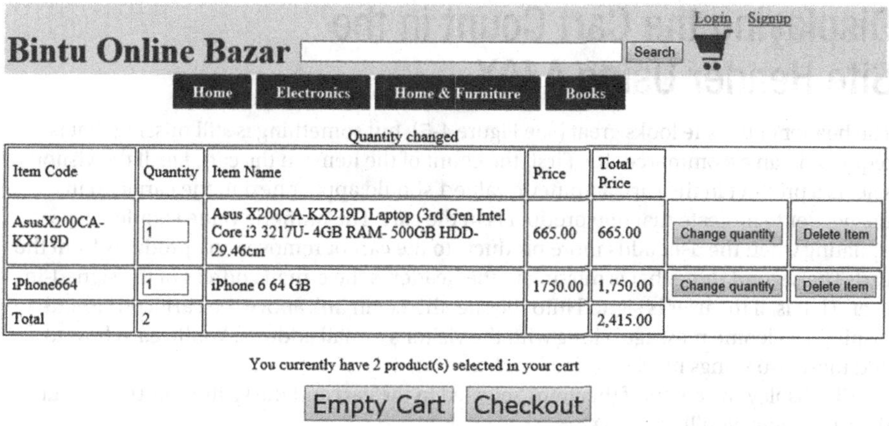

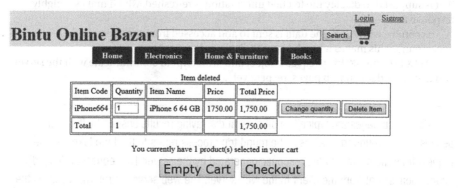

Figure 4-4. *Cart's content after changing the quantity of any item in the cart*

You can also delete any product from the cart by selecting the Delete Item button in that respective row. After deleting the Asus laptop from the cart, for example, only one item will be left in the cart, as shown in Figure 4-5.

Figure 4-5. *Cart's content after deleting an item from the cart*

The Empty Cart button at the bottom will delete all the items from the cart. You will get a message confirming this action, as shown in Figure 4-6.

Figure 4-6. *The mesaage you see when the cart is empty*

Displaying the Cart Count in the Site Header Using AJAX

The header of the site looks great (see Figure 4-5), but something is still missing that is required in an e-commerce site. First, the count of the items in the cart, i.e., if the visitor selects a product in the cart, a numeric value 1 should appear next to the cart icon in the header to indicate that one product is in the cart. The numeric value should keep updating when the user adds more products to the cart or removes any products from the cart. The second thing that is missing in the header is the e-mail address of the signed-in user. That is, if the user is signed into the site, the Login link above the cart icon should display a welcome message, along with the visitor's e-mail address. You'll learn how to add these two things now.

To display the count of the items selected in the cart and the visitor information in the site header, you'll use AJAX.

AJAX stands for Asynchronous JavaScript and XML. It is an umbrella term used for creating dynamic and highly responsive web pages. Usually, in a web application, partial updating of a web page is not possible. For example, when the user prompts for some information from the database on the server, the entire web page is refreshed to display the fetched information. That is, even if the fetched information is meant to be displayed in a small region of the web page, the entire page is reloaded. With AJAX, only the region that is supposed to display the fetched information is refreshed, which makes it highly responsive.

Secondly, with AJAX, the data is sent to and accessed from the server in the background. This makes it much faster at displaying responses.

AJAX uses the XMLHttpRequest object and JavaScript to communicate with the server and to display data on web pages, respectively.

■ **Note**   Web pages are typically a bit slow at displaying results desired by the users because of the round trip process. The round trip process refers to the time taken by the request from the client and the response generated by the server. The request of desired information is sent from the client to the web server. The web server, in return, accesses the required information from the database or processes it if required and sends it back to the client. The client reloads the entire web page to display the server's response. Even if the server's response is supposed to be displayed in a small region of the web page, the entire web page is refreshed. Whereas in AJAX, a small region of the web page can be refreshed, making it much faster at delivering results.

To display the count of items selected in the cart along with the visitor's e-mail address, the existing topmenu.php script is modified to appear as shown in Listing 4-3. Note that only the code in bold is new.

Listing 4-3. The topmenu.php Script Displays the Site Header That Indicates the Cart
Content and the User's Signed-In Status

```
<!DOCTYPE html>
<head>
<meta charset="utf-8">
<title>Bintu Online Bazar</title>
<link rel="stylesheet" href="css/style.css">
<script language="JavaScript" type="text/JavaScript">
function makeRequestObject(){
var xmlhttp=false;
try {
xmlhttp = new ActiveXObject('Msxml2.XMLHTTP');                        // #1
} catch (e) {
try {
xmlhttp = new
ActiveXObject('Microsoft.XMLHTTP');                                  // #2
} catch (E) {
xmlhttp = false;
}
}
if (!xmlhttp && typeof XMLHttpRequest!='undefined') {
xmlhttp = new XMLHttpRequest();                                      // #3
}
return xmlhttp;
}
function updateCart(){                                                // #4
var xmlhttp=makeRequestObject();
xmlhttp.open('GET',  'countcart.php', true);                         // #5
xmlhttp.onreadystatechange = function(){                             // #6
if (xmlhttp.readyState == 4 && xmlhttp.status == 200) {             // #7
var ajaxCart = document.getElementById("cartcountinfo");            // #8
ajaxCart.innerHTML = xmlhttp.responseText;
}
}
xmlhttp.send(null);
}
</script>
</head>
<body>
<table  width="100%" cellspacing="0" cellpadding="2">
<col style="width:30%">
<col style="width:40%">
<col style="width:20%">
<tr><td style="background-color:cyan;color:Blue;"></td><td
style="background-color:cyan;color:Blue;"></td><td
style="background-color:cyan;color:Blue;">
<?php
```

```php
if (session_status() == PHP_SESSION_NONE) {
session_start();
}
if (isset($_SESSION['emailaddress']))
{
echo "Welcome " . $_SESSION['emailaddress'] .  "   ";   // #9
echo "<a href=\"logout.php\">Log Out</a></td></tr>";
}
else
{
echo "<a href=\"signin.php\">Login</a>   ";
echo "<a href=\"validatesignup.php\">Signup</a></td></tr>";
}
?>
<tr><td style="font-size: 35px;color:blue;background-color:cyan;">
<b>Bintu Online Bazar</b></font></td>
<td bgcolor="cyan">
<form  method="post" action="searchitems.php">
<input  size="50" type="text" name="tosearch">
<input  type="submit" name="submit" value="Search">
</form></td>
<td bgcolor="cyan" ><a href="cart.php"><img style="max-width:40px;
max-height:40px;width:auto;height:auto;" src="images/cart.png"></img>
<span id="cartcountinfo"></span></a>
</td></tr>
</table>
<div class="container">
<nav>
<ul class="nav">
<li><a href="index.php">Home</a></li>
<li class="dropdown">
<a href="index.php">Electronics</a>
<ul>
<li><a href="itemlist.php?category=CellPhone">Smart Phones</a></li>
<li><a href="itemlist.php?category=Laptop">Laptops</a></li>
<li><a href="index.php">Cameras </a></li>
<li><a href="index.php">Televisions</a></li>
</ul>
</li>
<li class="dropdown">
<a href="index.php">Home & Furniture</a>
<ul class="large">
<li><a href="index.php">Kitchen Essentials</a></li>
<li><a href="index.php">Bath Essentials</a></li>
<li><a href="index.php">Furniture</a></li>
<li><a href="index.php">Dining & Serving</a></li>
<li><a href="index.php">Cookware</a></li>
</ul>
```

```
</li>
<li><a href="index.php">Books</a></li>
</ul>
</nav>
</div>
<p>
```

Statement #1 creates an XMLHttpRequest object. The XMLHttpRequest object enables the JavaScript code to make asynchronous HTTP server requests. It is through using this object that you can make HTTP requests, receive responses, and update a region of the page completely in the background.

In order to make an HTTP request to the server using JavaScript, a class is required that was originally introduced in Internet Explorer as an ActiveX object. It's called XMLHTTP. JavaScript has a built-in XMLHttpRequest() function that can be used for making HTTP requests in other browsers, such as Firefox, Safari, and Opera.

Statement #1 tries to create an XMLHttpRequest object using ActiveXObject("Msxml2.XMLHTTP")and assuming that the browser is IE6+. If it fails, statement #2 executes ActiveXObject("Microsoft.XMLHTTP"), assuming the browser is IE5.0. If all these fail, the built-in function XMLHttpRequest() in statement #3 is used to create an XMLHttpRequest object.

The updateCart function shown in statement #4 defines a JavaScript function that displays the count of the items in the cart. This function is called whenever the user makes changes to the cart, i.e., whenever any item is added, modified, or deleted from the cart.

For implementing AJAX, the next task after creating the XMLHttpRequest object is to send the web request to get data from the server. The request is made using the open method. Statement #5 makes a request to the server with the GET method and passes the file name, countcart.php, to be executed on the server. The countcart.php script is shown in Listing 4-4 and it simply counts the number of rows in the cart table and returns the result.

■ **Note** All modern browsers—Chrome, IE7+, Firefox, Safari, and Opera—have a built-in XMLHttpRequest object.

When an asynchronous request is made to the server, you need to watch for the state of the request and also for the response to the request. To do this, a function called xmlhttp.onreadystatechange is used in statement #6 and it continuously checks the status of the request.

The readyState property shown in statement #7 holds the status of the server's response. Each time the readyState changes, the onreadystatechange function will be executed. Here are the possible values for the readyState property:

State Description

0 The request is not initialized

1 The request has been set up

2 The request has been sent

3 The request is in process

4 The request is complete

The status attribute in statement #7 represents the status of the HTTP request. If the status value is 500, it represents an Internal Server Error; a 400 value represents a Bad Request; 401 represents Unauthorized; 403 represents Forbidden; 404 is Not Found, and so on. The status value 200 means no error. The onreadystatechange function checks for the state of the request. If the state has the value of 4, that means that the full server response is received. If the status has a value of 200, that means the response doesn't have an error and you can continue processing it.

Statement #8 accesses the element with the cartcountinfo ID. The cartcountinfo is the ID of the span element that is added to the header after the cart icon. It is through this element that the cart count returned by the file countcart.php will be displayed.

Statement #9 displays the welcome message along with the user's e-mail address if the user is already signed in and the session variable exists. Also, if the user is signed in, statement #10 displays the Log Out link, which invokes the logout.phpfile when clicked.

To display the number of items in the cart, the countcart.php script, shown in Listing 4-4, accesses the items in the cart table that match the session ID of the site's visitor and returns the count of the rows fetched.

Listing 4-4. The countcart.php File Counts and Returns the Number of Items Selected in the Cart

```php
<?php
$totalquantity=0;
if (session_status() == PHP_SESSION_NONE) {
session_start();
}
$connect = mysqli_connect("localhost", "root", "gold", "shopping") or
die("Please, check your server connection.");
$sess = session_id();
$query="select * from cart where cart_sess = '$sess'";
$results = mysqli_query($connect, $query) or die(mysql_error());
while ($row = mysqli_fetch_array($results, MYSQLI_ASSOC)) {
extract($row);
$totalquantity = $totalquantity + $cart_quantity;
}
echo $totalquantity;
?>
```

You can see in this code that the connection to the MySQL server is established, the shopping database is active, and all the rows from the cart table that match the session ID of the visitor are accessed. The quantity of the items in the cart is added and the total of the quantity is returned as the cart count. Assuming the visitor selected two items in the cart, the cart count 2 will appear next to the cart icon in the site header, as shown in Figure 4-7.

Figure 4-7. *The web site header showing the count of items selected in the cart*

Upon clicking the Login link, the signin.php script is executed and it prompts the user to enter an e-mail address and password. If the user enters a valid e-mail address and password, a welcome message will be displayed in the header of the site as well as in the body of the page, as shown in Figure 4-8.

Figure 4-8. *The welcome message for the signed-in user is displayed in the site header*

Proceeding to Check Out

Once visitors are done adding items to the cart and want to purchase them, they can always click on the Checkout button found at the bottom of the cart (see Figure 4-7). When they click the Checkout button, the visitor's status is checked to determine whether they are signed in or not. To keep the shipment information for a product's delivery, the visitor needs to register with the site and must be signed in. If the visitor is not yet signed in, two links will be displayed—one that enables the user to sign in and another to create an account if the user has not yet registered. Depending on the current status of the visitors, they can either create a new account or sign in to the site.

The checklogin.php script shown in Listing 4-5 checks the login/sign in status of the visitor.

Listing 4-5. The checklogin.php Script Checks the Login Status of the Visitor

```php
<?php
include('topmenu.php');
if (session_status() == PHP_SESSION_NONE) {
session_start();
}
$connect = mysqli_connect("localhost", "root", "gold", "shopping") or
die("Please, check your server connection.");
$cartamount=0;
$cartamount = $_POST['cartamount'];
$_SESSION['cartamount']=$cartamount;
if (isset($_SESSION['emailaddress']))
{
$email_address=$_SESSION['emailaddress'];
echo "Welcome " . $email_address . ". <br/>";
}
if (isset($_SESSION['password']))
{
$password=$_SESSION['password'];
}
if ((isset($_SESSION['emailaddress']) && $_SESSION['emailaddress'] != "") ||
(isset($_SESSION['password']) && $_SESSION['password'] != "")) {
$sess = session_id();
$query="select * from cart where cart_sess = '$sess'";
$result = mysqli_query($connect, $query) or die(mysql_error());
if(mysqli_num_rows($result)>=1)
{
echo "If you have finished Shopping ";
echo "<a href=shipping_info.php>Click Here</a> to supply Shipping
Information";
echo " Or You can do more purchasing by selecting items from the menu ";
}
else
{
echo "You can do purchasing by selecting items from the menu on left side";
}
}
```

```
else
{
?>
<html>
<head>
</head>
<body>
<h3>Not Logged in yet</h1>
<p>
You are currently not logged into our system.<br>
You can do purchasing only if you are logged in.<br>
If you have already registered,
<a href="signin.php">click here</a> to login, or if would like to create an
account, <a href="create_account.php">click here</a> to register.
</p>
</body>
</html>
<?php
}
?>
```

As each user has her respective products chosen in her unique session, the session_start() function is invoked before reading the session variables. After that, connection to the MySQL server is established and the shopping database is selected. The e-mail address and password in the $_SESSION array are retrieved in case they were set by any web page earlier.

The $_SESSION array elements can only be set when the user is registered and has signed into the site; otherwise, its elements are not set. If the e-mail address and password is set in the $_SESSION array, i.e., if the user is already logged in, he is provided with two options. He must provide shipping information if he's finished shopping (see Figure 4-9) or he can continue shopping by selecting the category of items from the menu on top. But if the e-mail address and password are not set in the $_SESSION array, the user is asked to sign in or create an account.

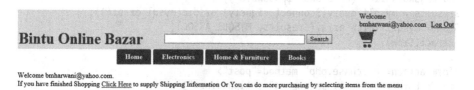

Figure 4-9. *The message displayed after checking the login status of the visitor*

Assuming the user is already registered, the next task is to supply shipping information for product delivery. You'll do that in the next section.

Supplying Shipping Information

If the user is already signed into the site, a link is shown to provide shipping information for product delivery. The shipping_info.php script shown in Listing 4-6 loads the address, state, country, and other information from the customer's table and displays it on the screen. Visitors can choose the same address for product delivery or can change it if required.

Listing 4-6. The shipping_info.php Script Enables Entering of Shipping Information for Product Delivery

```php
<?php
include('topmenu.php');
if (session_status() == PHP_SESSION_NONE) {
session_start();
}
if (isset($_SESSION['cartamount']))
{
$cartamount=$_SESSION['cartamount'];
}
$connect = mysqli_connect("localhost", "root", "gold", "shopping") or
die("Please, check your server connection.");
$email_address="";
if (isset($_SESSION['emailaddress']))
{
$email_address=$_SESSION['emailaddress'];
}
if (isset($_SESSION['password']))
{
$password=$_SESSION['password'];
}
if ((isset($_SESSION['emailaddress']) && $_SESSION['emailaddress'] != "") ||
(isset($_SESSION['password']) && $_SESSION['password'] != "")) {
$query = "SELECT * FROM customers  where email_address like '$email_address'
and password like (PASSWORD('$password'))";
$results = mysqli_query($connect, $query) or die(mysql_error());
$row = mysqli_fetch_array($results, MYSQL_ASSOC);
extract($row);
?>
<form action="purchase.php" method="post">
<table border="0" cellspacing="1" cellpadding="3">
<tr><td colspan="2" align="center">Your information available with us:</
td></tr>
<tr><td>Email Address:</td><td><input size="20" type="text"
name="email_address" value="<?php echo $email_address; ?>"></td></tr>
<tr><td>Complete Name: </td><td><input size="50" type="text"
name="complete_name" value="<?php echo $complete_name; ?>"></td></tr>
```

```
<tr><td>Address:   </td><td><input size="80" type="text" name="address1"
value="<?php echo $address_line1; ?>"></td></tr>
<tr><td></td><td><input size="80" type="text" name="address2" value="<?php
echo $address_line2; ?>"></td></tr>
<tr><td>City:   </td><td><input size="30" type="text" name="city"
value="<?php echo $city; ?>"></td></tr>
<tr><td>State:   </td><td><input size="30" type="text" name="state"
value="<?php echo $state; ?>"></td></tr>
<tr><td>Country:   </td><td><input size="30" type="text" name="country"
value="<?php echo $country; ?>"></td></tr>
<tr><td>Zip Code:   </td><td><input size="20" type="text" name="zipcode"
value="<?php echo $zipcode; ?>"></td></tr>
<tr><td>Phone No:   </td><td><input size="30" type="text" name="phone_no"
value="<?php echo $cellphone_no; ?>"></td></tr>
<tr><td colspan=2 align="center">Please update shipping information if
different from the shown below: </td></tr>
<tr><td>    Address to deliver at:   </td><td><input type="text" size="80"
name="shipping_address_line1" value="<?php echo $address_line1; ?>"></td></tr>
<tr><td></td><td><input type="text" size="80" name="shipping_address_line2"
value="<?php echo $address_line2; ?>"></td></tr>
<tr><td>    City:   </td><td><input size="30" type="text"
name="shipping_city" value="<?php echo $city; ?>"></td></tr>
<tr><td>    State:   </td><td><input size="30" type="text"
name="shipping_state" value="<?php echo $state; ?>"></td></tr>
<tr><td>    Country:   </td><td><input size="30" type="text"
name="shipping_country" value="<?php echo $country; ?>"></td></tr>
<tr><td>    Zip Code:   </td><td><input type="text" size="20"
name="shipping_zipcode" value="<?php echo $zipcode; ?>"></td></tr>
<tr><td><input type="submit" name="submit" value="Supply Payment
Information"></td><td>
<input type="reset" value="Cancel"></td></tr>
</table>
</form>
<?php
}
?>
</body>
</html>
```

The session is started. The connection is established with the MySQL server and the shipping database is selected. The e-mail address and password entered during the sign-in operation and stored in the $_SESSION array are retrieved and assigned to the $email_address and $password variables.

A SQL statement is executed to retrieve all the details of the visitor (including name, address, city, state, country, ZIP code, and phone number) from the customers table. This information is displayed on the screen. The shipping information is also displayed. Visitors can get the product's delivery using the address that was already provided while creating the account or they can provide new shipping information. After supplying the shipping information, the visitor can click on the Supply Payment Information button to pay for the products.

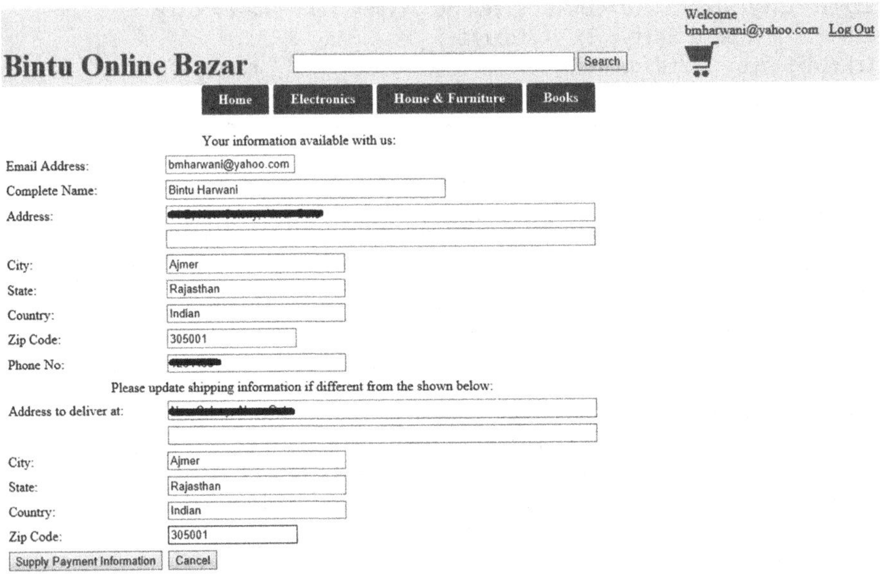

Figure 4-10. Entering shipping information for the products

You have now come to the stage in your web site where you want the users to pay for their items. In the next section, you'll learn about the different payment modes.

Understanding Different Payment Modes

In e-commerce sites, payments for purchased products are processed electronically. The main electronic payment modes are:

- **Credit Cards**—A credit card is small plastic card issued by a bank or some provider that enables its holder to purchase goods or services on credit. The card issuer puts a credit limit and the card holder cannot spend more than that. When a card holder purchases something, the card issuer pays on behalf of the card holder. The card holder then pays the amount back to the card issuer after a specific time period.

- **Debit Cards**—A debit card, like a credit card, is a small plastic card that enables the card holder to pay from his bank account. The card holder first needs to put money into his bank account and then can pay for the purchased goods or services via the debit card. The major difference between debit and credit cards is that when you use a debit card, the amount is deducted from your bank account immediately. There must be sufficient funds in your bank account for the transaction to go through. Where as, in the case of credit cards, even if there is insufficient funds in the account, the transaction is completed and the bank pays on behalf of the customer.

- **Smart Cards**—Similar to credit and debit cards in appearance, the smart card has a small microprocessor chip embedded in it. It stores the customer's information along with the monetary information. The monetary information is updated when the customer makes purchases.

- **E-Money**—In this mode of payment, the amount is transferred from one financial body to another directly, without involvement of any card company in the middle.

- **Electronic Fund Transfer**—This is an electronic payment method that transfers money from one bank account to another. Fund transfer can be done using ATMs (Automated Teller Machines) or using a computer. To transfer funds on a computer, the customer needs to register on the bank website. After signing in, they can make a request to transfer a certain amount to the seller's account. The bank transfers the amount to the specified account if it is in the same bank; otherwise, the request is transferred to ACH (Automated Clearing House).

- **Cash on Delivery Transactions (COD)**—The payments in this mode are made directly from the customer to the seller.

- **Netbanking**—The customer using this method pays money to the e-commerce site from their accounts by supplying a netbanking ID and PIN. No card is required for this method of payment.

■ **Note**   E-commerce sites collect money from consumers through a service provider known as a *payment gateway* provider. A payment gateway is an e-commerce application service provider that processes credit card and other card payments. It acts as a bridge between the consumer who is making purchases and the bank that issued the credit card. Payment gateways provide a safer platform for money exchanges to take place. In cash on delivery (COD) transactions, payment gateway is not involved because the payments are made directly from the customer to the seller.

Making Payments

After choosing products to purchase, the next step is to pay for them. The purchase.php script prompts the visitor to supply payment information.

To accept payments online through credit and debit cards, you can use several online payment processing services. I am using the 2CheckOut.com service in my purchase.php script, as shown in Listing 4-7. Visit https://www.2checkout.com/ to learn more.

JQUERY

The code shown in Listing 4-7 makes use of jQuery, so let's take a quick look at jQuery.

jQuery is a lightweight, feature-rich JavaScript library. It makes it easier to apply JavaScript on your site. In fact, many complex tasks like traversing HTML elements, implementing animation, handling events, etc. can be easily applied to your site just by using jQuery methods. Here are a few of jQuery's features:

- jQuery makes it quite easy to select DOM elements and manipulate them as required.

- jQuery is capable of sensing different events on HTML elements and then taking actions accordingly.

- jQuery enables you to apply AJAX to your site, thus making it highly responsive.

- jQuery includes several built-in animation effects that can be directly applied to your site.

- jQuery is supported by most major browsers, including IE 6.0+, FF 2.0+, Safari 3.0+, Chrome, and Opera 9.0+.

Listing 4-7. The purchase.php Script Enables You to Enter Payment Mode and Shipping Information

```
<HTML>
<HEAD>
<script type="text/javascript" src="https://www.2checkout.com/checkout/
api/2co.min.js"></script>
<script src="//ajax.googleapis.com/ajax/libs/jquery/1.11.0/jquery.min.js"></
script>
<script>
var successCallback = function(data) {
var myForm = document.getElementById('payment-form');
// Set the token as the value for the token input
myForm.token.value = data.response.token.token;
myForm.submit();
};
```

```
// Called when token creation fails.
var errorCallback = function(data) {
// Retry the token request if ajax call fails
if (data.errorCode === 200) {
call  tokenRequest();
} else {
alert(data.errorMsg);
}
};
var tokenRequest = function() {
// Setup token request arguments
var args = {
sellerId: "102626791",
publishableKey: "EOF6517A-CFCF-11E3-8295-A7DD28100996",
ccNo: $("#card-number").val(),
cvv: $("#card-cvc").val(),
expMonth: $("#card-expiry-month").val(),
expYear: $("#card-expiry-year").val()
};
// Make the token request
TCO.requestToken(successCallback, errorCallback, args);
};
$(function() {
// Pull in the public encryption key for our environment
TCO.loadPubKey('production');
$("#payment-form").submit(function(e) {
// Call our token request function
tokenRequest();
// Prevent form from submitting
return false;
});
});
</SCRIPT>
</HEAD>
<BODY>
<?php
if (session_status() == PHP_SESSION_NONE) {
session_start();
}
if (isset($_SESSION['cartamount']))
{
$cartamount=$_SESSION['cartamount'];
}
$complete_name=$_POST['complete_name'];
$address1 = $_POST['address1'];
$city = $_POST['city'];
$state = $_POST['state'];
$zipcode = $_POST['zipcode'];
```

```
$country = $_POST['country'];
$shipping_address_line1 = $_POST['shipping_address_line1'];
$shipping_address_line2 = $_POST['shipping_address_line2'];
$shipping_city = $_POST['shipping_city'];
$shipping_state = $_POST['shipping_state'];
$shipping_country = $_POST['shipping_country'];
$shipping_zipcode = $_POST['shipping_zipcode'];
$phone_no= $_POST['phone_no'] ;
$_SESSION['complete_name'] =$complete_name;
$_SESSION['address1'] =$address1;
$_SESSION['city'] =$city;
$_SESSION['state'] =$state;
$_SESSION['zipcode'] =$zipcode;
$_SESSION['country'] =$country;
$_SESSION['shipping_address_line1'] =$shipping_address_line1;
$_SESSION['shipping_address_line2'] =$shipping_address_line2;
$_SESSION['shipping_city'] =$shipping_city;
$_SESSION['shipping_state'] =$shipping_state;
$_SESSION['shipping_country'] =$shipping_country;
$_SESSION['shipping_zipcode'] =$shipping_zipcode;
$_SESSION['phone_no'] =$phone_no;
?>
<span class="payment-errors"></span>
<form action="placeorder.php" method="POST" id="payment-form" >
<input id="token" name="token" type="hidden" value="">
<table border="0" cellspacing="1" cellpadding="3">
<tr><td colspan="2" align="center">Online Payment Form</td></tr>
<tr><td>Card Number</td><td><input type="text" size="20" autocomplete="off"
id="card-number"></td></tr>
<tr><td>CVC</td><td><input type="text" size="4" autocomplete="off"
id="card-cvc"></td></tr>
<tr><td>Full Name</td><td><input type="text" id="name" size="80"
autocomplete="on"></td></tr>
<tr><td>Expiration (MM/YYYY)</td><td><input type="text" size="2"
id="card-expiry-month"><input type="text" size="4" id="card-expiry-year"></td></tr>
<tr><td>Amount to Pay: </td><td><?php echo $cartamount; ?></td></tr>
<tr><td colspan="2" align="center"><input type="submit" name="submit"
value="Submit" onclick="formSubmit()">
</table>
</form>
</BODY>
</HTML>
```

Upon running the script, the user is asked to provide credit/debit card information, as shown in Figure 4-11.

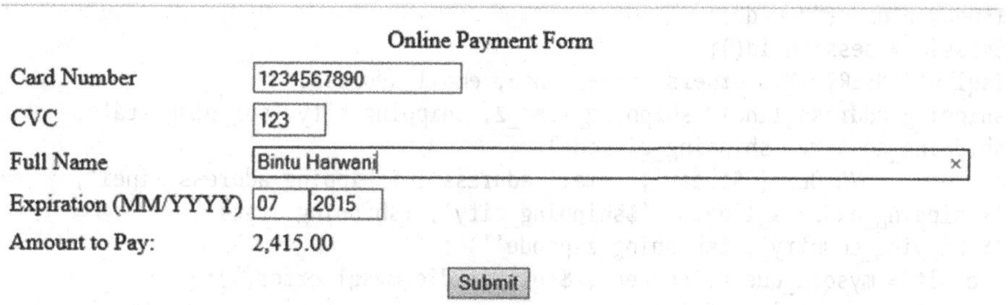

Online Payment Form

Card Number	1234567890
CVC	123
Full Name	Bintu Harwani ✕
Expiration (MM/YYYY)	07 2015
Amount to Pay:	2,415.00

Submit

Figure 4-11. Entering payment information

When the user clicks the Submit button, the order will be placed and information about the purchased products will be saved in the orders and orders_details tables. The placeorder.php script shown in Listing 4-8 accepts the visitor's order and displays the order number along with a "thanks" message.

Listing 4-8. The placeorder.php Script Places the Order

```php
<?php
require_once("lib/Twocheckout.php");
Twocheckout::privateKey('E0F6517A-CFCF-11E3-8295-A7DD28100996');
Twocheckout::sellerId('102626791');
include('topmenu.php');
if (session_status() == PHP_SESSION_NONE) {
session_start();
}
if (isset($_SESSION['cartamount']))
{
$cartamount=$_SESSION['cartamount'];
}
$connect = mysqli_connect("localhost", "root", "gold", "shopping") or
die("Please, check your server connection.");
$complete_name=$_SESSION['complete_name'];
$address1 = $_SESSION['address1'];
$city = $_SESSION['city'];
$state = $_SESSION['state'];
$zipcode = $_SESSION['zipcode'];
$country = $_SESSION['country'];
$shipping_address_line1 = $_SESSION['shipping_address_line1'];
$shipping_address_line2 = $_SESSION['shipping_address_line2'];
$shipping_city = $_SESSION['shipping_city'];
$shipping_state = $_SESSION['shipping_state'];
$shipping_country = $_SESSION['shipping_country'];
$shipping_zipcode = $_SESSION['shipping_zipcode'];
$phone_no= $_SESSION['phone_no'] ;
$email_address= $_SESSION['emailaddress'] ;
```

```
$today = date("Y-m-d");
$sessid = session_id();
$sql = "INSERT INTO orders (order_date, email_address,
shipping_address_line1, shipping_line_2, shipping_city, shipping_state,
shipping_country, shipping_zipcode)
            VALUES ('$today','$email_address','$shipping_address_line1',
'$shipping_address_line2', '$shipping_city','$shipping_state',
'$shipping_country','$shipping_zipcode'')";
$result = mysqli_query($connect, $sql) or die(mysql_error());
$orderid = mysql_insert_id();
try {
$charge = Twocheckout_Charge::auth(array(
"merchantOrderId" => "$orderid",
"token" => $_POST['token'],
"currency" => 'USD',
"total" => '$cartamount',
"billingAddr" => array(
"name" => '$complete_name',
"addrLine1" => '$address1',
"city" => '$city',
"state" => '$state',
"zipCode" => '$zipcode',
"country" => '$country',
"email" => '$email_address',
"phoneNumber" => '$phone_no'
),
"shippingAddr" => array(
"name" => '$complete_name',
"addrLine1" => '$shipping_address_line1',
"city" => '$shipping_city',
"state" => '$shipping_state',
"zipCode" => '$shipping_zipcode',
"country" => '$shipping_country',
"email" => '$email_address',
"phoneNumber" => '$phone_no'
)
), 'array');
if ($charge['response']['responseCode'] == 'APPROVED') {
echo "Thanks for your Order!";
echo "Please, remember your Order number is $orderid<br>";
echo "<h3>Return Parameters:</h3>";
echo "<pre>";
print_r($charge);
echo "</pre>";
$query = "SELECT * FROM cart WHERE cart_sess='$sessid'";
$results = mysqli_query($connect, $query) or die(mysql_error());
while ($row = mysqli_fetch_array($results, MYSQLI_ASSOC)) {
extract($row);
```

```
$totalamount=$totalamount + ($cart_price * $cart_quantity);
$sql2 = "INSERT INTO orders_details (order_no, item_code, item_name,
quantity, price)
VALUES ($orderid,$cart_itemcode,'$cart_item_name',
$cart_quantity,$cart_price)";
$insert = mysqli_query($connect, $sql2) or die(mysql_error());
}
$sql2 = "INSERT INTO payment_details (order_no, email_address,
customer_name, payment_type, name_on_card, card_number, expiration_date)
VALUES ($orderid,$cart_itemcode,'$cart_item_name',
$cart_quantity,$cart_price)";
$insertpayment = mysqli_query($connect, $sql2) or die(mysql_error());
$query = "DELETE FROM cart WHERE cart_sess='$sessid'";
$delete = mysqli_query($connect, $query) or die(mysql_error());
session_destroy();
}
} catch (Twocheckout_Error $e) {
print_r($e->getMessage());
}
?>
```

The session is started. Connection to the MySQL server is established and the shopping database is selected. The shipping information (such as the shipping address, city, state, country, ZIP code, and payment mode entered by the user in the shipping_info.php script) is retrieved from the $_POST array. A SQL statement is executed to store that information in the orders table along with the system date, which is the date the order was placed. In the orders table a primary key field called order_no is made. It is of integer type and is set to auto_increment mode, which means its value is automatically incremented by 1 on insertion of every record. With the help of the following statement:

```
$orderid = mysql_insert_id();
```

The id of the order_no of the inserted record in the orders table is retrieved and is stored in the $orderid variable. This order number is added to each item in the orders_details table to determine all the items that have been purchased with a particular order number.

All the records in the cart table with the given session ID (of the same user) are extracted one by one and stored in the orders_details table. After that, all the items from the cart table with the given session ID are deleted. The user sees the "Order Acceptance" message and the order ID is displayed for future communication. In the end, the session is destroyed.

Summary

In this chapter, you saw how the chosen products are saved in the cart table, which keeps track of the visitor's session ID. Also, you saw how the cart content is managed and modified as the visitor makes changes. You also saw how the site's header displays the cart count and the visitor's sign-in status. Finally, you learned to supply the shipping information, accept payments, and save the chosen products into the orders and orders_details tables. You learned about different types of payment modes.

The goal of the book was to learn about different PHP statements and functions and their practical implementation in making a fully featured e-commerce site. In this book, you learned how information about the customers and products can be saved into the MySQL database for future use. You now know how a drop-down menu is made and how it can be used in linking other web pages of the site.

You saw how the most crucial and important component of an e-commerce site, the shopping cart, is defined, how the items are chosen in it, and how they can be manipulated. You also learned about the different payment modes through which an e-commerce site can accept payments from its customers.

In this book, I tried to keep the code as simple as possible and each script is supported with explanations and with the output. I hope you have enjoyed reading the book and have learned the concepts deeply enough to make your own fully featured e-commerce site.

Index

Get the eBook for only $5!

Why limit yourself?

Now you can take the weightless companion with you wherever you go and access your content on your PC, phone, tablet, or reader.

Since you've purchased this print book, we're happy to offer you the eBook in all 3 formats for just $5.

Convenient and fully searchable, the PDF version enables you to easily find and copy code—or perform examples by quickly toggling between instructions and applications. The MOBI format is ideal for your Kindle, while the ePUB can be utilized on a variety of mobile devices.

To learn more, go to www.apress.com/companion or contact support@apress.com.

Printed in the United States
By Bookmasters